# Piano Chords Two
## (All Sharp and Flat Keys)

A Beginner's Guide To Simple Music Theory
and Playing Chords To Any Song Quickly

## MICAH BROOKS

PUBLISHING | EST. 1985

## Also By Micah Brooks

The Piano Authority Series:

*Piano Chords One:*
*A Beginner's Guide To Simple Music Theory*
*and Playing Chords To Any Song Quickly*


The Guitar Authority Series:

*Worship Guitar In Six Weeks:*
*A Complete Beginner's Guide to Learning*
*Rhythm Guitar for Christian Worship Music*

*42 Guitar Chords Everyone Should Know:*
*A Complete Step-By-Step Guide To Mastering*
*42 Of The Most Important Guitar Chords*

*Guitar Secrets Revealed:*
*Unconventional and Amazing Guitar Chords,*
*Professional Techniques, Capo Tricks,*
*Alternate Tunings, Head Math, Rhythm & More*


Songbooks and Music:

*Micah Brooks All Things New EP Songbook*

*Micah Brooks All Things New EP*

Devotional Books:

*21 Day Character Challenge:*
*A Daily Devotional and Bible Reading Plan*

*Galatians: A Fresh, New Six Day*
*Bible Study and Commentary*

*Ephesians: A Fresh, New Six Day*
*Bible Study and Commentary*

*James: A Fresh, New Five Day*
*Bible Study and Commentary*

Marriage and Family Books:

*Forsaking All Others:*
*The book we wish we'd had when dating,*
*engaged, and in the early years of our marriage*
*to set us up for future success.*

# Copyright Information

# Dedication

I am delighted to dedicate *Piano Chords Two* to the newest addition in our family, Levi. Levi loves to dance–more than any baby we've had. In fact, I can make a simple beatbox with my mouth and he will bop around the room. Levi, perhaps one day you will use this book as a jumpstart for your music career. Your mom, brother, sisters, and I love you from the bottom of our hearts.

# Contents

# Introduction

## It's time to tickle all the black keys

If you've finished my first book, *Piano Chords One*, then hello again! I'm hoping that you've just completed it and you're rip-roaring and ready to get started on this next one. If that's you, awesome! Even if you haven't been through the first book in this series, don't fret! You'll still be set in motion to learn each and every important flat and sharp chord and their fingerings. If you discover that you aren't following along as well as you'd like, please read *Piano Chords One*. In it you'll find the basic piano techniques that good musicians need. Beyond learning the chords themselves, you'll also find an explanation of chord theory and an intro to understanding how to read sheet music. It's all in there. Now, onto *Piano Chords Two*.

This is important: you can move too slowly when learning an instrument. I'll repeat, you can move too slowly when you first set out to learn an instrument. Whether you may able to move too quickly isn't being discussed here. What I'm getting at is if you are a perfectionist, you will need to do your best to learn to let yourself fail. Failing is a part of learning. Wayne Gretzky may have said it best, "You miss one hundred percent of the shots you don't take". Perfectionists are their own worst enemy. If you are one, you must overcome yourself. You must allow yourself to fail. Don't take yourself too seriously. Take my word on this. I am a recovering perfectionist. I'm giving you a *get out of your own way* card. It's free, but you must take and use it.

Before we launch into our first key–which happens to be the key of B♭–please look over the next chapter called *The Foundation*. Like any foundation that a structure sits upon, this chapter will give you the front end information you'll need as you work through each key in this book. Now, onward!

Micah Brooks

# The Foundation

## Fundamentals that work in every key

Before we can get info our first flat or sharp chord we need to work through some of the fundamentals. If you've read *Piano Chords One*, then you are ahead of the game. Use this chapter as a review. If you are a newcomer to learning piano chords through my method, please make sure you use the following information.

## Right-hand

The vast majority of people are right-handed. While that may mean that righties have a hand up [get it] on the piano–as melodies and many of the notes on the piano are played with the right-hand–to play well, you'll need both hands to cooperate with one another.

First, we need to assign numbers to each of your fingers of your right-hand. Beginning with your thumb, we count one through five, ending with your pinky. Your thumb is one (R1); index finger is two (R2); middle finger is three (R3); ring finger is four (R4); the pinky finger is five (R5). See the diagram below.

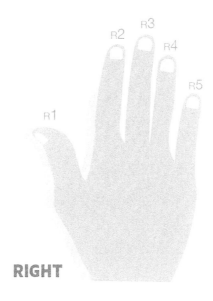

RIGHT

# Left-hand

While right-handed people begin with an advantage–as in they are doing more with their dominant hand–left-handed people tend to gain the advantage as they play more difficult pieces on the piano. Lefties have more dexterity in the hand that performs the root notes for each chord. This means that if you're left-handed, you may naturally be able to place your fingers in more difficult positions than right-handed people.

Notice that your left-hand is the mirrored opposite of your right. If you hold them both in front of your face, you'll see that your thumbs are beside each other and are numbered the same. We begin the left-hand numbering as we did with the right. Your thumb is one (L1); index finger is two (L2); middle finger is three (L3); ring finger is four (L4); the pinky finger is five (L5). See the diagram below.

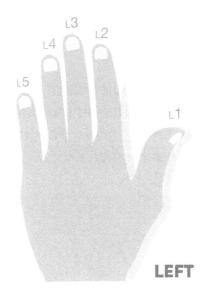

# The tennis ball test for good posture

Now that we have your fingers numbered, it's time to sit down at your piano. In my lessons, I keep a tennis ball in the room. For the first lesson, I have my student sit at the piano and place their fingertips onto the keys. Next, I'll put the tennis ball into the palm of their right and then left-hands. It forces the wrists to stay up while curling the fingers. This is the proper form when playing the piano. It doesn't need to be exaggerated and it can change slightly based on what type of chord or melody you are playing, but it is an excellent posture. You'll be able to better stretch your fingers for more difficult chords. Plus, you'll be able to play for longer sessions without needing to take a break because your hands hurt. For some, this will even help if you have arthritis or carpal tunnel. As you progress, you'll learn when this posture is critical and when you can relax it a bit. I recommend beginning with the tennis ball test every time that you sit down to play during the first few weeks. It will help you establish good habits.

# Let's answer a few important questions

So, you're now sitting at the piano and we've made sure you have good posture. It's time to learn a bit about music theory. If you understand these next few concepts, they'll be the foundation for every chord and key that you'll play. Since we haven't talked about what a chord or key is yet, let's begin there.

# What is a chord?

A chord is built as several notes played simultaneously. This can be as few as two notes or as many as your fingers can press down at one time. In fact, with the addition of the damper pedal (which is the sustain pedal at the foot of your piano), you can hold down every key on the piano at one time if you'd like. It won't sound pleasant, but you could do it.

Most chords are made of two, three, four, or five notes. The chords we will learn in this book are built as three notes. When a single note is played on the piano it is distinct. The ear hears it and knows that it is a single note. The human voice, the trumpet, trombone, snare drum, and flute are among some of the instruments that only play one note at a time. These are called monophonic instruments. Polyphonic instruments include the piano, guitar, bass guitar (even though it rarely plays many notes at one time), and the harmonica. Each allows more than one note to be performed at a time.

Chords that are made of three notes are called triads. The prefix *tri* means three. Because three notes are played together, our ears cannot easily distinguish the individual notes. Instead, they blend them together to create a rich sound. Chords make for the perfect accompaniment underneath a vocal or lead instrument, like the sound of a rhythm guitar. You may have heard of one guitarist being called the rhythm player and the other lead. The rhythm player is typically playing chords while the lead player primarily plays single notes.

## What is a key and what's a major scale?

I imagine that you've heard of the key of "C" or playing a "C" scale. A key is a group of seven notes, or pitches, that have a unique relationship to one another. This is especially true when played in series, which is known as a scale. For our purposes, we are going to speak about major scales. As you sit down to play your piano, notice the note in the very middle. It's called *middle C*. It's a white key that is directly before a set of two black keys. See the diagram below.

MIDDLE "C"
-Location On The Piano-

From middle C, we continue up a full step, which means that we skip the half step note, which is a black key in this case. That new note is D. We continue another full step to E. Then, we jump only a half step. There is no black key in between E and F. This means that the half step we need to play is F. Next, we add three more full steps, remembering that half steps are black keys in this case and we are omitting them. The correct notes are G, A, and B. As we continue on, we end up back on a C, but eight notes higher than where we started. That eight note jump is called an octave. The term octave has the prefix *oct* which means eight. To recap, a major key and the scale we just made began on our foundation note–or tonic note as it is sometimes called, which is C, and then moved up in this series of jumps: full step, full step, half step, full step, full step, full step, half step. This made the C scale, which is also all of the notes in the key of C Major: C, D, E, F, G, A, B, and C. See the diagram below.

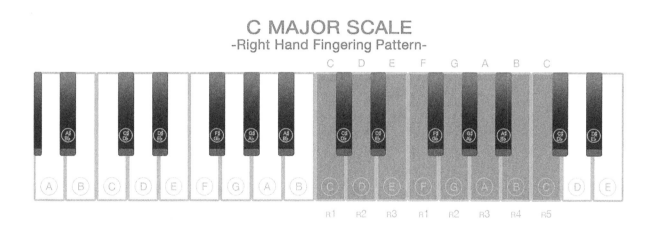

## C MAJOR SCALE
-Right Hand Fingering Pattern-

# How to play a scale with both of your hands

We've already assigned numbers to our fingers and now know what notes are in a scale. Let's add the two together to talk about which fingers to use when playing scales. Our hands only have five fingers, but there are eight notes we'd like to play in this scale. At least three fingers are going to be used twice. This is how you play the C scale with the right-hand.

C = R1; D = R2; E = R3 [Then your thumb, R1, moves under your middle finger, R3]; F = R1; G = R2; A = R3; B = R4; C = R5.

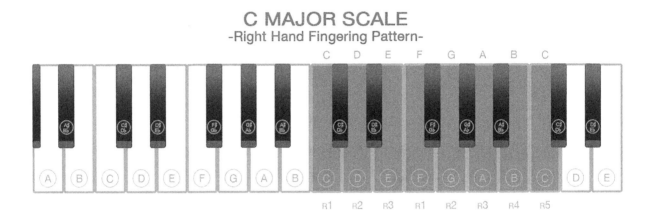

The left-hand pattern is similar to the right, but not exactly the same. While we won't go over left-hand finger position in each key in this book, you can use the following as a template. Please know, some keys require the left-hand to differ slightly from this particular pattern. You should either use your best judgment or refer to the Appendix in the back of this book. This is where I have outlined all major keys–including all natural and flat/sharp keys–with fingering patterns for both hands.

C = L5; D = L4; E = L3; F = L2; G = L1 [Then your middle finger, L3, moves over your thumb, L1] A = L3; B = L2; C = L1.

When playing a scale with the right-hand, your thumb goes under your middle finger to finish the series. When using the left, your middle finger goes over your thumb to finish the series. Once you are able to play both scales independently, using the thumb-under or middle finger-over technique, try to play both hands at the same time. If you move slowly, you'll be able to do both scales simultaneously. At first, it's a bit like trying to pat your head and rub your tummy, but soon you'll get the hang of it.

# Sheet music basics

While I promised you that we weren't going to get into reading sheet music, we have to learn a little bit about it to be prepared to play chords and songs. No, we're not about to lean into Beethoven or Bach. These are the fundamentals that you'll be glad you know going forward. Likely, you've seen some of this before.

### Staff, clef, key and time signatures, and measures

Music is laid out on five lines called the staff. Included on the staff are three elements: the clef, key signature, and time signature. The most common two clefs are the treble clef, which looks like a squiggly "G", and the bass clef, which looks like a hook with two dots. The bass clef is also known as the "F" clef. While it's not always true, typically the right-hand plays the notes on the treble (upper) clef, while the left plays those on the bass (lower) clef. For our purposes in this book, we will only discuss notes on the treble clef. Melodies are usually written on the treble clef, so you'll be able to play songs using that clef without needing to know the bass clef at this time.

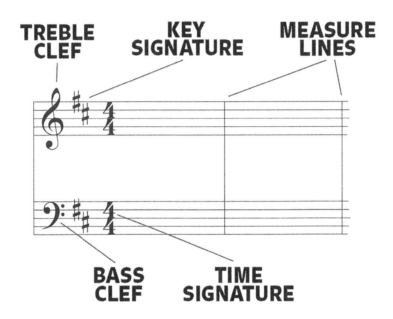

Key and time signatures are variable elements that change per song. Key is flats and sharps written as ♯ and ♭ on their proper note lines. We will discuss several keys. Time signature is written as two numbers. Some common time signatures include 4/4, 6/8, and 3/4. You will find vertical lines that separate sections along the staff. These are called measure lines. Like lines on a football field, measure lines make it easy to organize written music and to delineate what's coming next.

Music is usually built on "4's". In common time, known as 4/4 time–and in which most pop and worship songs are played–you'll count in repeating sets of four. This means that all note durations in each measure need to total four when you add up all the notes held within them. We are getting to that, but let's speak first about notes.

## EGBDF and FACE

There are two pneumonic devises that people have used for ages to remember the notes on the treble clef. The first is **E**very **G**ood **B**oy **D**oes **F**ine and it stands for each note on the treble clef that is found on a line. It's not the coolest phrase ever, but it is memorable and may be helpful. The other is **F.A.C.E.** The notes in between the lines on the treble clef spell the word *face*. There is no need to come up with a separate pneumonic device in this case since face is already a word. Use both as you memorize the notes on the treble clef. The notes below the staff are C, which has a line through it, and D, which has no line. The two notes above the staff are G, which has no line, and A, that does have a line through it.

## Whole Note and Whole Rest

The whole note is represented by a ring with no stem. It's the longest note in common time, being held for four full beats. I tell my younger students that it looks like a tomato. A whole rest also has a four-beat duration. A rest assumes that you will not play anything for the amount of time that is designated by the rest.

## Half Note and Half Rest

The half note is held half as many beats as the whole note, thus the name *half*. You hold a half note and half rest for two beats. A half note is represented as a ring with a stem.

## Quarter Note and Quarter Rest

A quarter note is held for one-fourth as many beats as the whole note. It is also half of a half note. We're getting confusing now with our math, so I'll stop explaining it that way. Quarter notes are the most common note you'll use early on and are represented by a darkened ring with a stem. A quarter rest is also common and represented by a squiggly line.

## Eighth Note and Eighth Rest

The eight note is, you guessed it, held for an eighth of the amount of a whole note. Eighth notes are faster sounding than quarter notes. It takes eight of them to fill a common time measure. They look like a quarter note, but there is an additional flag atop of the stem. The eighth rest also has a flag on top.

## Sixteenth Note and Sixteenth Rest

As you have figured out by now, a sixteenth note is held a sixteenth of a whole note. Sixteenth notes are even faster sounding than eighth notes. Sixteenth notes look like eighth notes, but with two flags. A sixteenth rest also has two flags on top.

## Tied and Dotted Notes

The final note types that we need to discuss are tied and dotted notes. They both serve similar functions. Tied notes are two notes joined together by a curved line, which is known as a tie. The tie acts to add the two note durations together, equaling one new note duration. A dotted note is similar to a tied note, but a dotted note is always counted as the note duration itself plus half. A dotted note is represented as a note with a small dot beside it.

Let's use an example to understand them both because there are instances when they mean the same thing and others when only one can be used. Let's suppose we tie a quarter note to a half note. This means one beat (the quarter note) is tied together with two beats (the half note). The note being played now totals three beats and is held as long. We can also arrive at this same duration using a dotted note. If we have a dotted half note, the half note is already held two beats plus the addition of one more beat–which is half of the half note. This new note duration is held for three beats.

The two notes differ in that a dotted note cannot be held across a measure line and can only form a few durations. A tied note could technically be held as long as the player would like or until you run out of sheet music to print it upon.

## Everything hinges on understanding chord root positions and their inversions.

Now that we have all of that technical music jargon out of the way, let's get to the fun stuff. Each and every chord that you will learn has three positions. I tell my students that water has three states: solid, liquid, and gas. In all three states, water's molecular structure is the same. The following is true for chords. Chords have three notes in them. For our purposes, we are going to speak about a major chord. Later in the book we will cover a few more complex chords.

All major chords are built using the first, third, and fifth notes in the major scale with the first note being the root note. As you'll see, you can arrange them in any order you'd like and they'll still add up to the same chord, but in different positions. These new positions are called inversions. Inversions are the lifeblood of the pop/rock/worship keyboardist. They sound amazing and are not all that hard to play. Soon, you'll be mastering all of your chords in root position and using their inversions.

# Root position

When you play any chord with the root note as the lowest note, it's called root position. Some other names for this include, the tonic chord, home base, and even just *the chord.* Root position assumes that you are playing the first, third, and fifth notes together at one time and in that order. Most people begin by learning all of their chords in root position. While this isn't bad, it's not efficient. Because the piano is a wide instrument, playing all chords in root position means that your hand is flying all over the keyboard to reach chords that are distances apart. We will not only learn our chords in root position, but we will make sure to learn their first and second inversions right away. The benefit of root position is that the tonic (root) note is played on the bottom of the chord and the top note is the fifth note of the scale. Every diagram in this book includes the fingering positions for the right-hand that are indicated using an "R" in front of each finger number. Plus, you'll find one root note to be played using the left-hand. Every instance of the left-hand has an "L" beside the finger number. Here is a C chord diagrammed in root position.

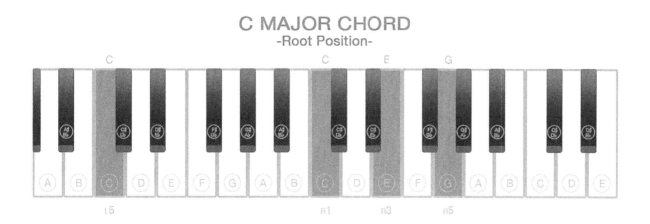

C MAJOR CHORD
-Root Position-

# First inversion

When we restructure our chord a little bit we find our first inversion. Instead of playing our major chord using the first, third, and fifth notes of the scale, we transport the first note above the fifth (it's technically now the eighth note of the scale). Our major chord now reads: third, fifth, and first (again, it's the eighth note of the scale, which an octave repeat of the root note). The benefit of this inversion is that the tonic (root) note is now being played at the top of the chord. For songs with melodies that use the root note quite a bit this inversion is helpful. The downside is that the root note is no longer on the bottom of the chord. In this case, you'll need to supply the root note with your left-hand. Notice that your pinky finger (L5) is still playing the same low C note that it was while playing the C chord in root position. This strengthens the low end of the chord since the inversion has moved the stronger sounding root note, C, to the top of the chord. Here is the C chord diagrammed in its first inversion.

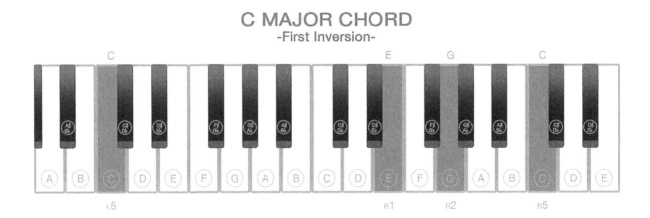

C MAJOR CHORD
-First Inversion-

# Second inversion

The second inversion is the final position to learn. What we've rearranged with the first inversion we'll do again with the second. Moving the third note to the top, now we have these three notes making up our major chord: fifth, first, and third. Having the third note on the top of the chord adds a richness to the sound being played. As with the first, the second inversion requires the left-hand to play the root note. Notice that there will be at least five notes distance between your left-hand root note and your right-hand performing the second inversion. This spacing can be helpful when you want your chords to sound somewhat spaced apart. Here's the C chord using the second inversion. Notice the top note is now E.

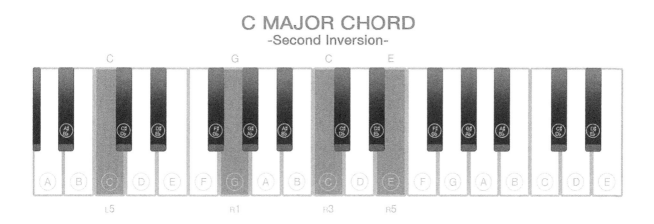

C MAJOR CHORD
-Second Inversion-

# Numbers: Music theory at its core

Music is math. While music definitely has an artsy side, at its core, it's math. One plus one always equals two. Even the most unique songs played by the oddest musicians are still performing something that can be quantified. All music follows some rules. Of course, it breaks these rules from time to time too. Known in Nashville, Tennessee as the Nashville Numbers System, all chords live on a chords scale designated by numbers. If you don't live in Nashville, you just call these *numbers*. You could say this is music theory at its core. Let's discuss what simple music theory is.

# Chords scale and how it works in every key

Much like the major scale from the previous section, chords walk up the scale as single notes do. They are as follows: 1, 2m, 1/3, 4, 5, 6m, 5/7, 1. A 1 chord is the tonic chord. This is home base and it sounds like it. Our ears long for a 1 chord. The 2m is the first minor chord we come to–pronounced *2-minor*. Minor chords are sad sounding counterparts to major chords. The 2m lifts from the 1 chord. The 1/3 chord is the first fractional chord we come to. This means that you have a 1 chord with the third note in the scale shifted up as its bass note. It continues to lift the progression upward. The 4 and 5 chords are our other two major chords along the chords scale. They are definite sounding and easy to hear. A 4 chord is relaxed while a 5 chord is more dominant in nature. They each lift to the 6m. The 6m is the second minor chord along the scale. While the 2m always wants to lift up to the next one–such as a 4 chord or back to a 1–the 6m can stand on its own. It's about as strong to our ears as a 1 chord. The final chord along our chords scale is the 5/7. The same as the 1/3, the 5/7 is a fractional chord. It includes a 5 chord with the seventh note shifted upward as its bass note. Typically, this chord is used as a passing chord, which means that you use it to transition to another chord and won't play it for long durations. This is basic music theory used for creating and playing pop songs. It may be confusing as simply a theory, but will make the most sense as you learn to play these chords on the piano.

# The circle of fifths and how this book is laid out.

Before we launch out into the deep of our first key, it may be interesting to note that I haven't laid out this book to go from the keys of A♭ to B♭ then to C♭ (a key which we won't even learn–you'll see why in just a minute) and so on. Instead, it's laid out using the circle of fifths. This means that we will learn the key of B♭ which has two flats. Then we'll continue to add flats as we move leftward on the circle until we reach G♭ (known as well as F#). This will give you seven new keys in which to play. There are two sets of keys that are nearly identical to one another, but you'll still be glad you took the time to learn this way. As a small side note, the key of C♭ is almost always called the key of B so I do not go over that key in this book. Also, most musicians prefer D♭ and G♭ to C# and F#. While I've never encountered the key of C# in the real world, guitarists tend to like the key of F# rather than G♭. It's their preference, but G♭ is still the standard.

## CIRCLE OF FIFTHS

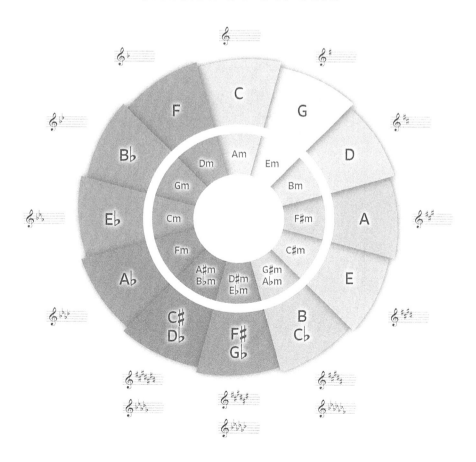

# The Key of B♭

## What you need to know about the key of B♭

Before we even set sail, I need to disclose one quick fact. Technically speaking, the first key that includes a flat note is the key of F, but it's also a natural-note key. It was covered in chapter three of *Piano Chords One*. In case you were hoping to learn that key, please reference that book. Building from the key of F–which lowered the B natural note to a B♭–we'll now produce the key of B♭ by taking the E natural note down a half step to an E♭. Below you can see what notes form the B♭ scale and how to finger that scale with your right-hand.

## Notes in the key of B♭ and fingering the scale

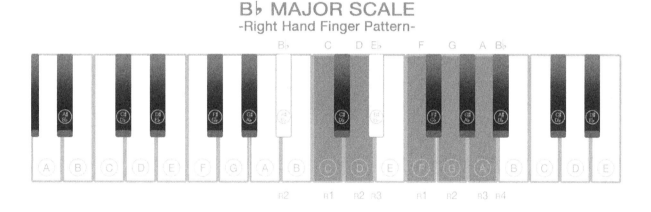

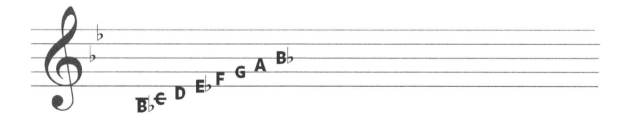

# B♭ chord and its inversions

We will not review the definition of chords and inversions in each chapter, but here's a reminder. In order to be proficient in any key, knowing which chord inversion to use is critical. The following sections teach you the positions using your right-hand to play the B♭ chord and the chords that are related to it. These include all three fingering positions: root position, then first and second inversions. They are equally important. Please be sure you know them well. The B♭ chord in the key of B♭ is the 1 chord. This makes sense as the 1 chord is always built from the root note of the key.

Also, notice that I gave you a single root note (also called the tonic note) to play with the left-hand. This stabilizes the chord you are playing by having a lower note played to strengthen the bottom of the chord. While this note isn't required to play the chord, it does make it sound better. With each of these chords, I've recommended that you use the pinky (L5) on your left-hand. It makes for a great starting place for future left-hand usage. However, you are welcome to use any of your left-hand fingers. You could even use a toe if you wanted to be weird. Here are all three positions of the B♭ chord.

## B♭ MAJOR CHORD
### -Root Position-

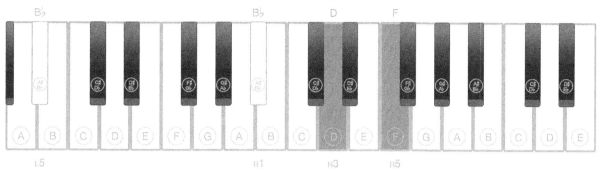

## B♭ MAJOR CHORD
### -First Inversion-

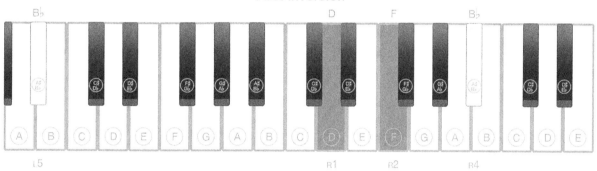

## B♭ MAJOR CHORD
### -Second Inversion-

# Cm chord and its inversions

The second step up from a B♭ major chord is Cm (pronounced *C minor*). Being only the first chord we come to after the root chord, B♭, Cm doesn't sound like we have drifted much from home base. It's because we haven't. Cm is the first minor chord we encounter. It sounds sad in comparison with the former major chord, B♭. You'll notice this distinction in every key when going from the 1 chord to a 2m, or B♭ to Cm in this case.

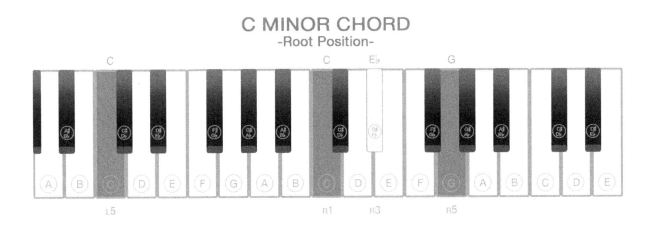

## C MINOR CHORD
### -Second Inversion-

# B♭/D chord and its inversions

The next stop along the B♭ chord scale is our first fractional chord. Remember, fractional chords are fundamental chords, like the 1 or 5 chord, but with the bass note shifted up. In this case, the bass note has been shifted up two steps from the note B♭ to a D. This gives the chord a lifting sense while keeping the tone happy. Another option for the third chord along this scale would be a 3m chord, or for this key, a Dm. The 1/3 is used far more often than a 3m for its upward motion and happier sound. 3m has a darker sound. That's why we'll learn the root position and inversions for the B♭/D here. However, you could learn the Dm chord in the first book, *Piano Chords One*, so you'd have both options to choose from if you want to hear the difference.

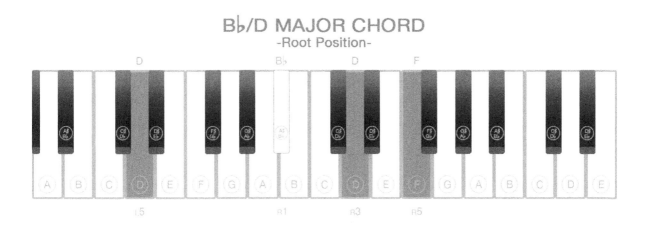

## B♭/D MAJOR CHORD
### -Root Position-

33

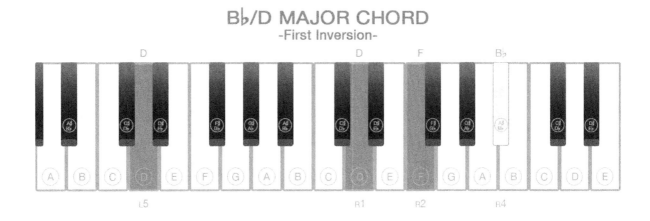

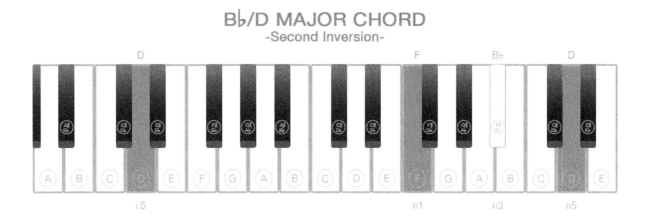

## E♭ chord and its inversions

The E♭ chord is the fourth chord along the scale. It's the second of the three fundamental chords (1, **4**, and 5). You'll notice that the notes that make up an E♭ are almost identical those of a Cm. This will come in handy as you learn to transition from chord to chord. The difference between a Cm and an E♭ is that we've replaced the C note with a B♭. A 4 chord, or E♭ in this case, feels like it rises up from the 1 chord. It's almost unsettled until it moves back to 1. If you play a 1 chord, or B♭, and then move to the 4, E♭, you'll hear what I mean. Here's how to play all three versions of E♭.

## E♭ MAJOR CHORD
### -Root Position-

## E♭ MAJOR CHORD
### -First Inversion-

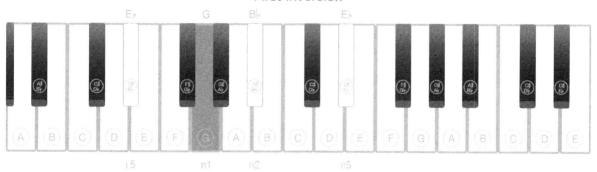

## E♭ MAJOR CHORD
### -Second Inversion-

# F chord and its inversions

F is the 5 chord in our series. The 5 chord is dominant. It doesn't sound like any other chord along the chord scale. It's often referred to as the dominant fifth. To the ear, it longs to move forward to a 1 chord or back to a 4. If you were to end a song on a 5, it would feel incomplete. Here's how to play the 5 chord, F.

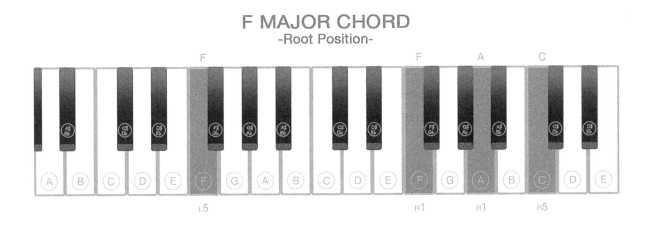

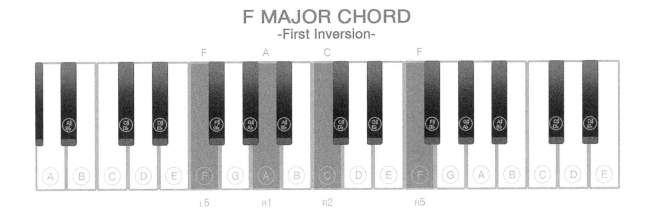

## F MAJOR CHORD
### -Second Inversion-

## Gm chord and its inversions

The 6m is the most dominant sounding minor chord you can play. It shares two of the same notes with the 1 chord, so you can imagine why it's so powerful. Songs often begin on a 6m rather than a 1 because it's more dramatic to the ear. The Gm is the 6m in the key of B♭.

## G MINOR CHORD
### -Root Position-

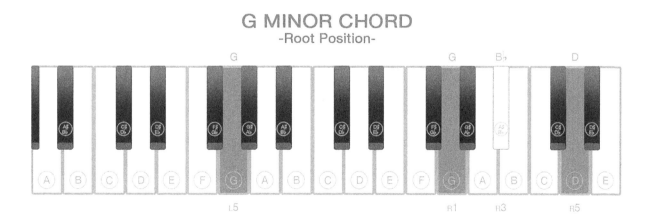

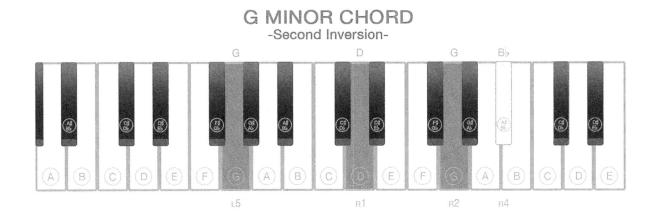

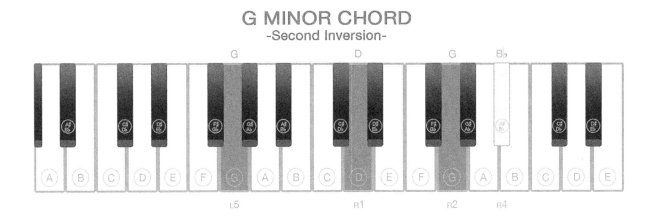

## F/A chord and its inversions

The last chord we'll learn in this key is the 5/7, or F/A. Built from a 5 chord, F, the bass note is shifted up two full steps, making it a 7 note, or A. If you play Gm to F/A, you'll hear the lifting nature of the F/A. It's another chord that would be strange on which to end a song. Here's how to play your root position and inversions of F/A.

## F/A MAJOR CHORD
### -Root Position-

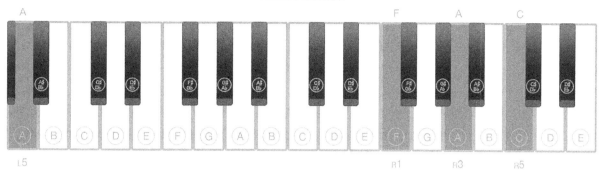

## F/A MAJOR CHORD
### -First Inversion-

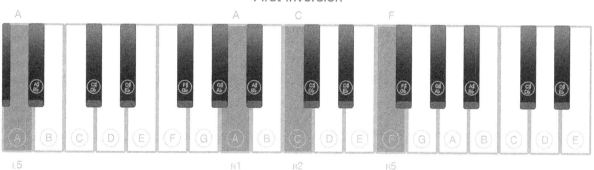

## F/A MAJOR CHORD
### -Second Inversion-

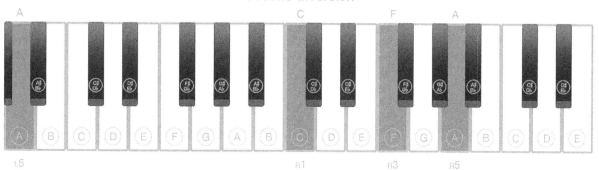

# Practice progressions

It's time for some practice measures (you could even call these songs if you are feeling spunky). Move slowly and take your time as you learn them. You are welcome to use a metronome with a slower BPM (beats per minute) such as 55BPM. A metronome is a musician's best friend–and most hated foe. Even if you aren't familiar with the word, you've likely heard the in-time clicks of a metronome coming from somewhere. Metronomes provide a series of clicks or ticks that are programmed to a selected rate. 50-90 beats per minute would be fairly slow, while 90-150BPM would be rather fast. If you do not own a metronome, you can download several metronome apps for free to your smartphone, tablet, or computer.

### Playing chords in root position

Now, let's move on to the good stuff. If you play each of these chord series solely in root position, you'll be sounding great, but playing inefficiently. Let's begin by only using root position and then we'll put our inversions to the test.

## Chord patterns using root position

The following three rhythm examples are some of the most popular chord patterns you'll find. You may even find them in some of your favorite songs. The first pattern is likely the most famous: 1, 5, 6m, 4. While you play it, hear if you can recognize it as the chord pattern for one of your favorite tunes. We will use all three of these chord patterns throughout the rest of this book. The only thing that should change is the key in which you are playing. Hopefully, this will help you make a connection between chords, numbers, keys, and how they all integrate one to another.

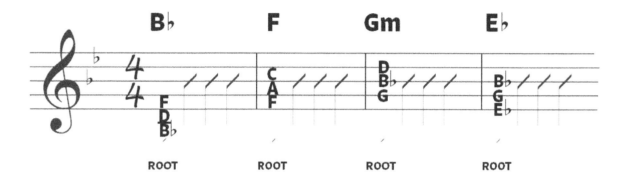

The next pattern does not begin with a 1 chord. However, it is still in the key of Bb. The first chord in a song does not determine the key. It's the number of flat or sharp notes that determines the key. Since there are two flats in this one–Bb and Eb–we are still in the key of Bb. This pattern is 2m, 1, 6m, 5.

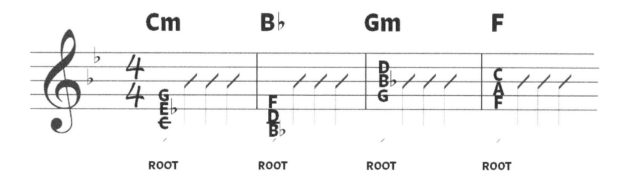

41

The final progression that we will go over in each chapter is 1, 4, 5, 6m. There are thousands of more progressions you could play. We are learning a few of the most common and using the same ones in each chapter so that we notice continuity. As you play this one you may find that as each chord moves to the next it feels like it is moving upward. There is a lifting motion to this pattern.

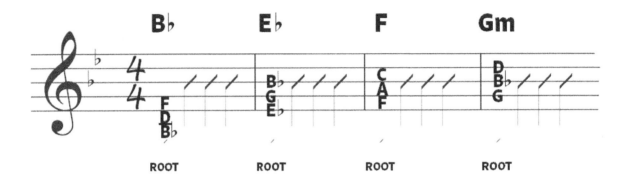

# Let's use our inversions

Now it's time to put some of our inversions to good use. As you played the chords solely in root position so far, hopefully, you've noticed how much your right-hand had to move across the keys. For some of the progressions, your right-hand moved more than ten or twelve inches. As you'll see next, inversions, used in the right shape, make transitioning chords easier. They also sound more connected as the notes are closer together.

One of the best ways to train your hands to stay within inversion boundaries is to set up a few bumpers. In the diagram below, I've placed pencils on the lower A and upper B♭ keys. These act like bumpers in a bowling alley or lines on a road that keep you safe as you drive a car. While these aren't required, I recommend using them as you learn how to shape your fingers for each progression. I know they have helped all of my students perform at a higher level.

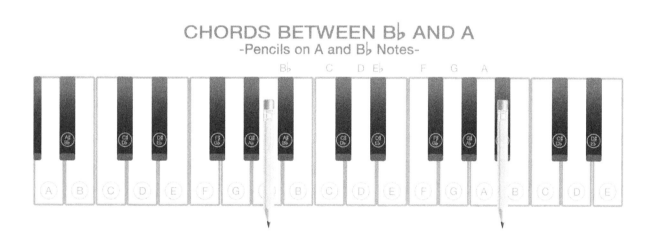

CHORDS BETWEEN B♭ AND A
-Pencils on A and B♭ Notes-

Finally, all of the patterns that are shown are transcribed for your right-hand only. It's assumed that you will play the root note of each chord with your left-hand as well. This means that for the first progression, B♭, F, Gm, E♭, your left-hand should play the notes: B♭, F, G, and E♭. While I recommend using your pinky finger, L5, of your left-hand, try a few of these using other fingers as well.

## Playing all chords between notes B♭ and A using root position and inversions

The first series keeps the 1 chord in root position while most of the others require inversions to stay within our boundary marker pencils. Don't forget to use your left-hand as well. It should play the root note of each of these chords.

## Playing all chords between notes D and C using root position and inversions

Let's move our pencils from the A note up two to the C and move the B♭ pencil up two to a D. View the diagram below and then try to play the patterns using our new sets of inversions.

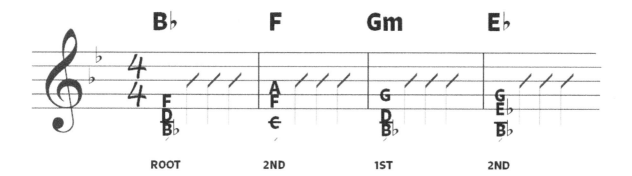

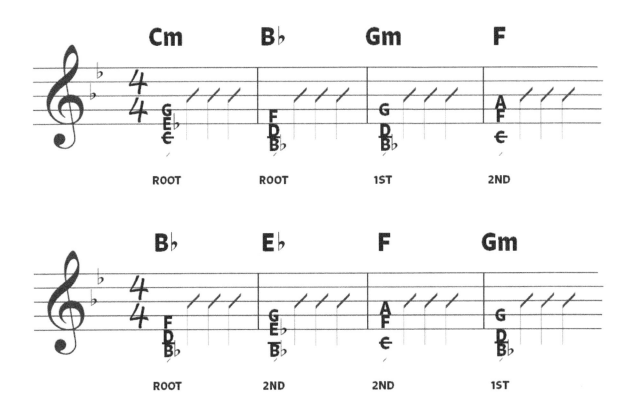

**Playing all chords between notes F and E♭ using root position and inversions**

In our final set of patterns in this chapter, move your pencils up two notes one more time. Now, place pencils on the E♭ and F notes. These progressions are the same as before but staying between these new note sets. Please notice that my diagram shows the pencils moving down an octave. You may want to do this, however, I'd recommend continuing to move your pencils upward if your piano or keyboard allows it. I only moved mine downward to fit neatly into this diagram.

## CHORDS BETWEEN F AND E♭
### -Pencils on E♭ and F Notes-

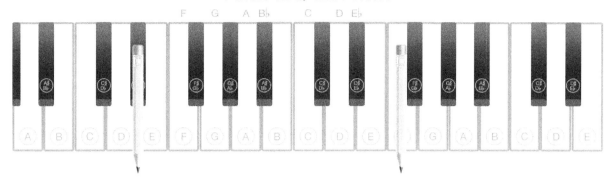

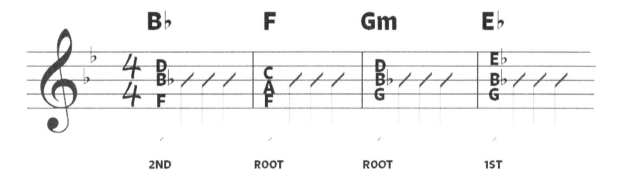

2ND        ROOT        ROOT        1ST

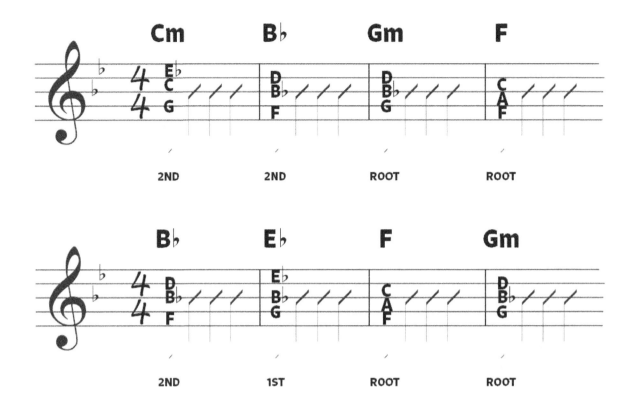

Before we move on to the key of E♭ that's next, the three patterns above are common, but are hardly the only ones you can use. In fact, we haven't even used the B♭/D or F/A chords. You could replace any of the B♭ or F chords in the previous progressions with our fractional versions. As you learn some of your favorite songs, you may find some of these progressions are those songs' backbones. Now, onward!

# The Key of E♭

## What you need to know about the key of E♭

The key of E♭ is the third tick to the left on the circle of fifths wheel from the key of C, which you learned about in the first chapter, *The Foundation*. We'll now add on an A♭ to our B♭ and E♭ notes. You will no longer play an A natural note. As we move along adding flats, the difficulty level increases. Don't let that slow you down. Each key has its own unique sound and is worth learning.

## Notes in the key of E♭ and fingering the scale

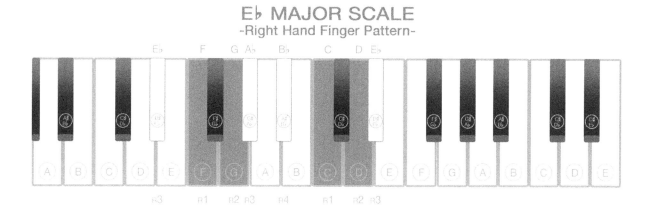

E♭ MAJOR SCALE
-Right Hand Finger Pattern-

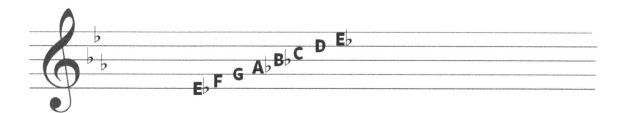

# E♭ chord and its inversions

As with the key of B♭, the 1 chord is always the root chord and, in this case, it's an E♭. You will likely recall that the E♭ chord was the 4 chord in the previous chapter and key. You'll play this E♭ the exact same way as you did before. Here's a reminder of how to play each of the E♭ positions in case you are coming to this chapter having skipped over the first.

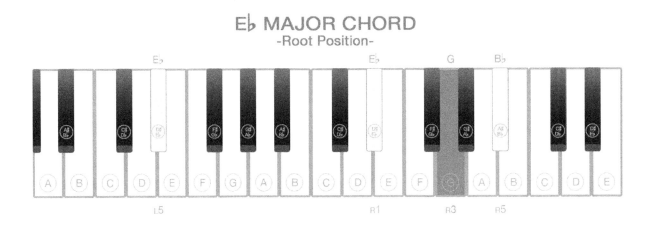

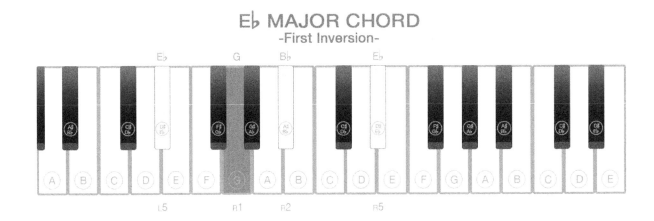

E♭ MAJOR CHORD
-Second Inversion-

## Fm chord and its inversions

Moving up, the 2m for the key of E♭ is Fm. This is the first time that you are playing this chord, but it is nearly the same as the F chord, which was the 5 chord in the previous key. The only difference is that the A natural note is flattened to an A♭. Here are all three positions.

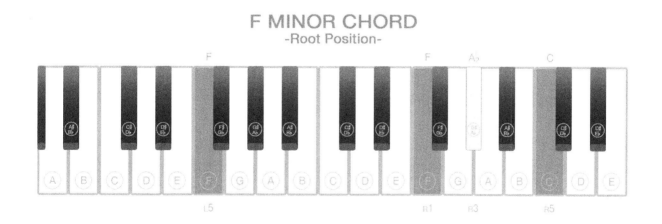

F MINOR CHORD
-Root Position-

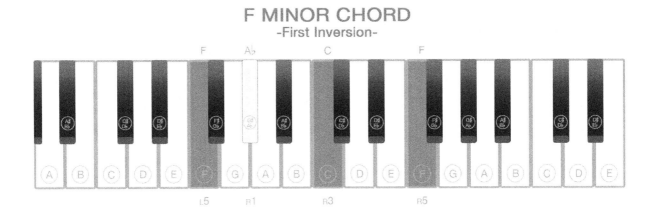

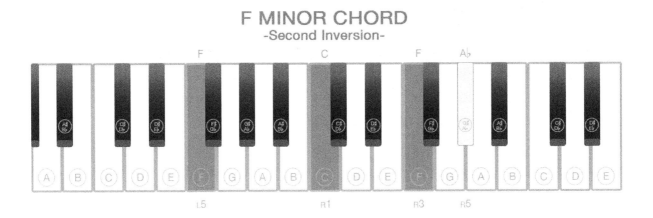

## E♭/G chord and its inversions

The 1/3 chord is E♭/G. Play this one the same way you did when you played the 1 chord, E♭, but move your left-hand from an E♭ note to a G. While the inversions are the exact same, I've created the fingering diagrams for this chord to begin an octave (eight notes) lower for the right-hand. The lowered octave may make it seem like it's in a different chord series, but the E♭ and E♭/G play the exact same. The only difference will be the up-shifted bass note.

## E♭/G MAJOR CHORD
### -Root Position-

## E♭/G MAJOR CHORD
### -First Inversion-

## E♭/G MAJOR CHORD
### -Second Inversion-

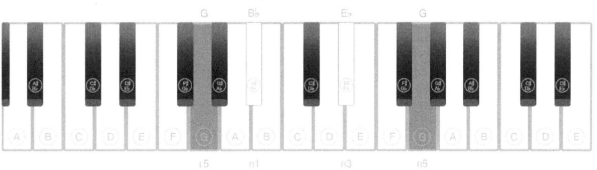

# A♭ chord and its inversions

The 4 chord in the key of E♭ is A♭. This is the first time we are seeing this chord. If you've worked through my first book in this series then you've played the similar chord A♭m. It was known as G#m then because it was the 6m chord in the key of B. The A♭ major chord is just like it, but you'll need to move your B note to a C. All of the inversions work just as they did with the G#m (A♭m). Here they are.

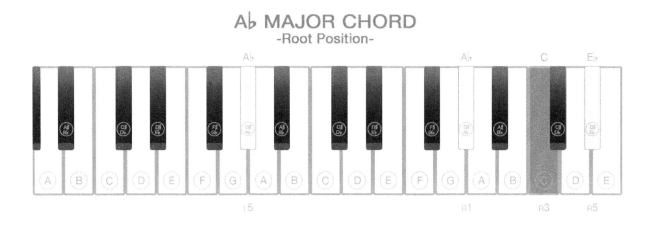

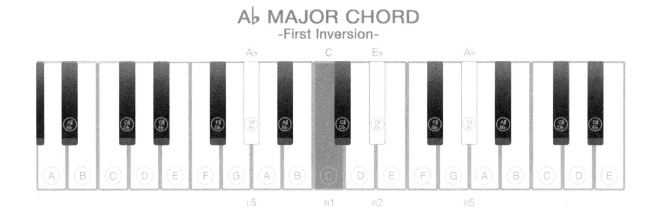

# B♭ chord and its inversions

The 5 chord is B♭. Remember, there is strength in a 5 chord. It also always sounds like it wants to go somewhere. It could be that it wants to go back to a 1, or E♭ in this key, or it could fall back to a 4, which is A♭. Since the B♭ was the first chord you learned in this book, you ought to be familiar with all three of these positions. Here they are again.

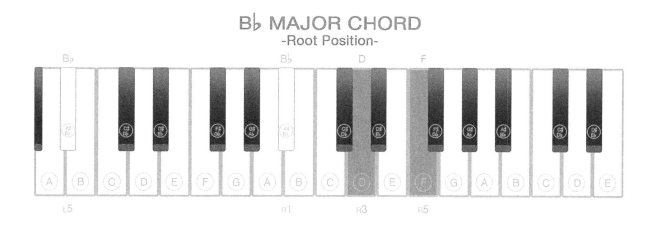

# Bb MAJOR CHORD
## -First Inversion-

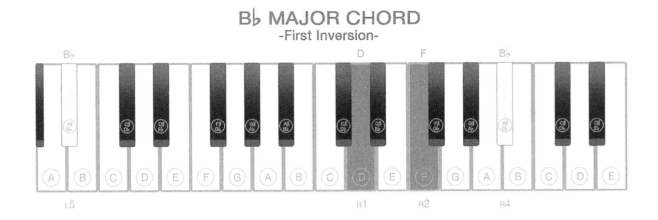

# Bb MAJOR CHORD
## -Second Inversion-

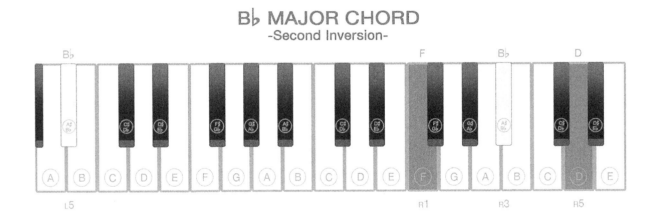

## Cm chord and its inversions

The Cm is the 6m chord in this key. This was the first minor chord we learned in this book. However, the Cm was the 2m in the key of Bb. Now, it's the 6m chord. You'll find the same chords performing different roles as you switch keys. It's what makes music fun and also interesting as you learn the fundamentals. Here are all three positions.

## C MINOR CHORD
### -Root Position-

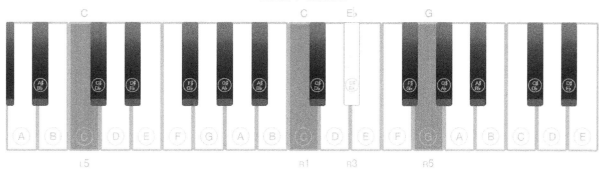

## C MINOR CHORD
### -First Inversion-

## C MINOR CHORD
### -Second Inversion-

# B♭/D chord and its inversions

The last chord in the key of E♭ is the 5/7, or B♭/D. B♭ and B♭/D are identical, only the bass note shifts up from B♭ to D. Moving between the two you should hear the sound of upward movement. The 5 always lifts to a 5/7. Here are all three versions.

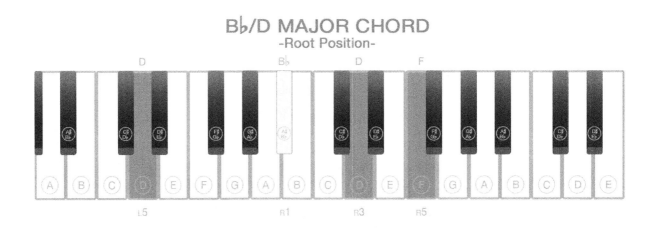

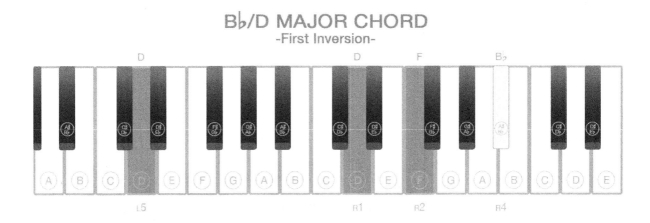

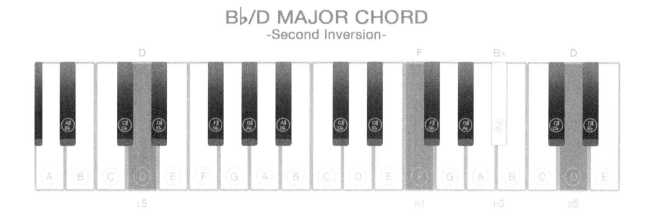

# Practice progressions

It's time for some practice measures. As before, you could even call these songs. Take your time learning them. Use a metronome with a slower BPM (beats per minute) such as 60 or 70BPM.

### Playing chords in root position

Here are all of your progressions with each chord played in root position. You should notice that they sound very similar to the ones you played in the key of B♭ because they are the same numbered progressions. For instance, the first progression is still 1, 5, 6m, 4. The difference is that you are now playing in the key of E♭ and you've added an A♭ note in place of the A natural.

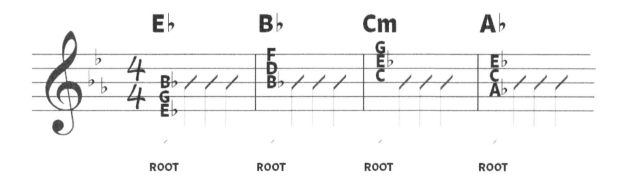

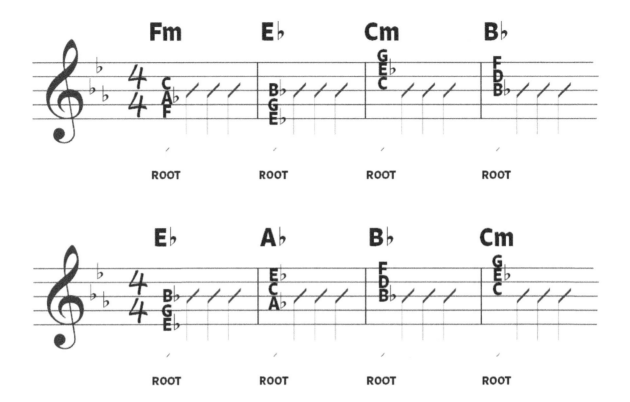

## Playing all chords between notes E♭ and D

As with the previous chapter, let's use pencils (or whatever bumper you have) as makeshift guardrails keeping you inside your inversion spacing. Let them act like a force field or an electric fence that you don't want to get close to. First, we'll begin by placing our pencils on the lower D and upper E♭ notes which will help us stay between the lower E♭ and upper D notes. We're using the same progressions above, only with the appropriate inversions. If you find your first pencil teetering because of the black key being raised, angle the pencil so that it has more stability.

# CHORDS BETWEEN E♭ AND D
## -Pencils on D and E♭ Notes-

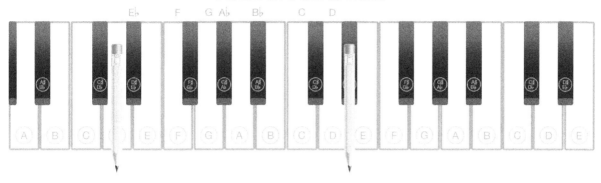

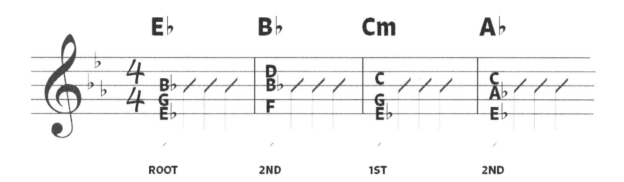

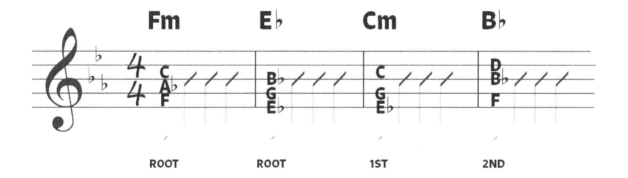

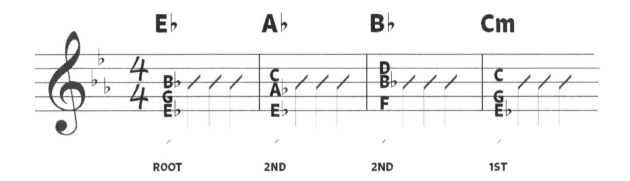

## Playing all chords between notes G and F

For our second set, move your pencils up to the F and G notes. This should keep all of your chords between the G and F notes on your piano.

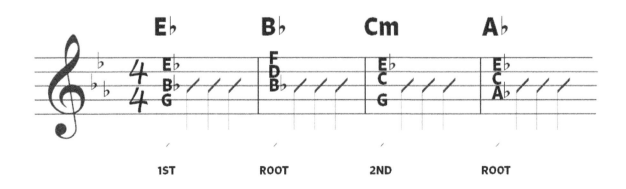

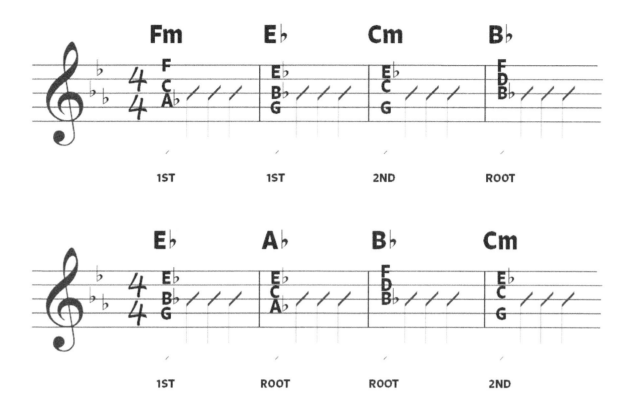

## Playing all chords between notes B♭ and A♭

Last, move your pencils up to the A♭ and B♭ notes. This final set keeps your right-hand fingers between B♭ and A♭. As an aside, this set uses the second inversion of the E♭ chord. This means that a G note is on the top of the chord each time you play the E♭. The G note is the third note in the E♭ scale. The third note of the scale is known as the color note of the chord. It's the note that adds the most definition to the chord. As you play through these progressions, notice each time you play the E♭ chord in its second inversion. There is a richness sounding from the top of the chord because of that third note, G, that's up there.

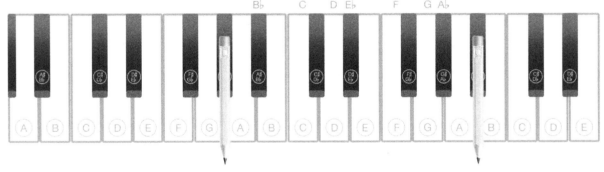

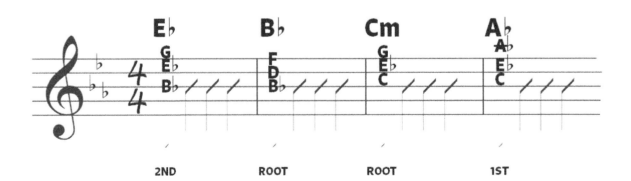

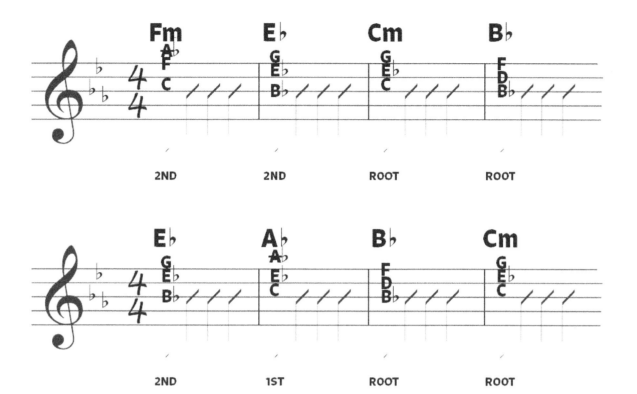

Micah Brooks

# The Key of A♭

## What you need to know about the key of A♭

Moving one tick to the left on the circle of fifths from E♭, we find the key of A♭. This is two ticks left from the key of B♭, from where we began. Continuing on from the last chapter–the key of E♭–we'll now add a D♭ note to the mix. This means that we are employing four black keys now. You may find the key of A♭ to be the most difficult so far. Don't let that slow you down. It's quite playable with practice.

## Notes in the key of A♭ and fingering the scale

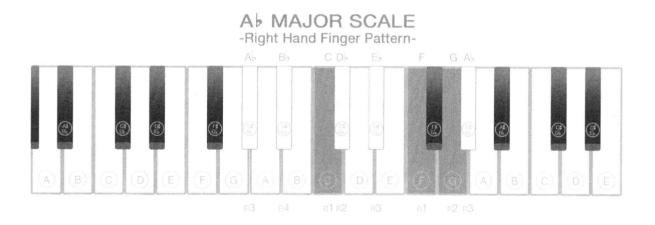

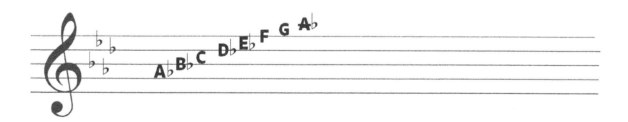

# A♭ chord and its inversions

By now you've probably figured out what each of the chords along the numbers scale should be. That being said, the key of A♭ begins with the 1 chord and is A♭. Here's how to play the A♭ chord. It is the exact same as you learned in the last chapter when you learned the 4 chord in the key of E♭, which is also A♭.

## A♭ MAJOR CHORD
### -Root Position-

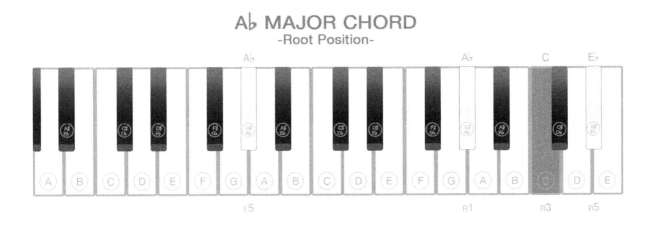

## A♭ MAJOR CHORD
### -First Inversion-

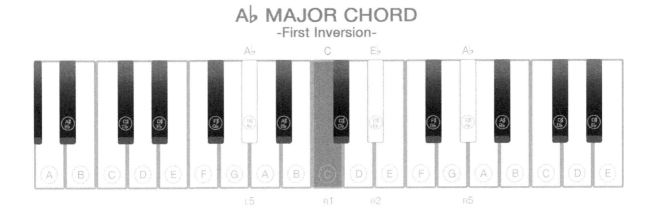

## A♭ MAJOR CHORD
### -Second Inversion-

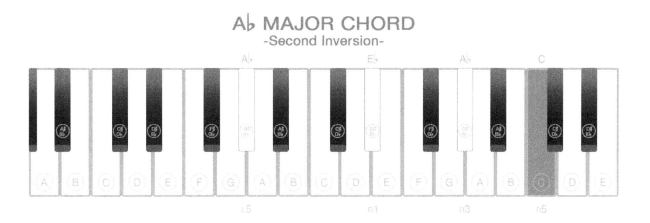

# B♭m chord and its inversions

The 2m chord is B♭m. Your right-hand will need to stretch to include the F note in each position for this chord. I recommend using the fingers suggested, but you can use whichever finger works best for you. Younger players with smaller hands should consider using your middle (R3) and pinky (R5) fingers to make each of these stretches. Your goal should be to play the chord whichever finger is closest to the preceding chord. The fingerings below are the ways that I naturally play them. Here's how to play each of the B♭m chords.

## B♭ MINOR CHORD
### -Root Position-

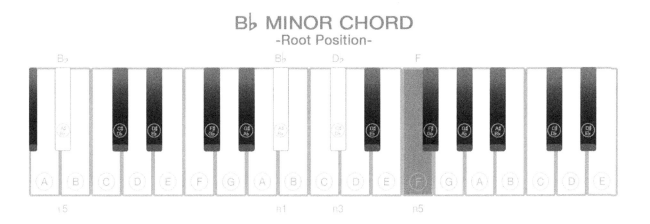

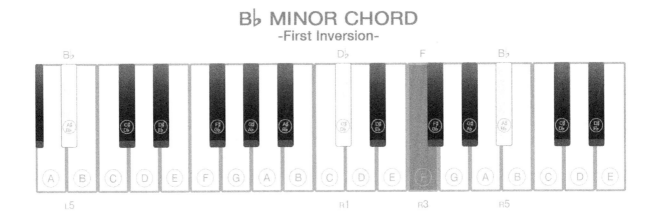

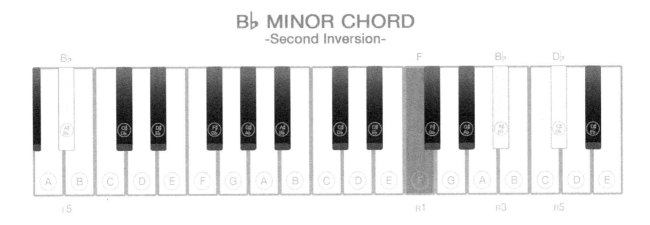

## A♭/C chord and its inversions

The 1/3 chord is A♭/C. You build it exactly as you have with the 1 chord, A♭, only move your left-hand from the root note, A♭, up to the third note of the scale, which is a C. Finger an A♭/C using the following diagrams.

## A♭/C MAJOR CHORD
### -Root Position-

## A♭/C MAJOR CHORD
### -First Inversion-

## A♭/C MAJOR CHORD
### -Second Inversion-

# D♭ chord and its inversions

Now let's move to the 4 chord, D♭. The D♭ chord and B♭m finger nearly the same, except that the B♭ note in each of your B♭m chords has been moved to an A♭ in each of these D♭ chords. Here's how to play them.

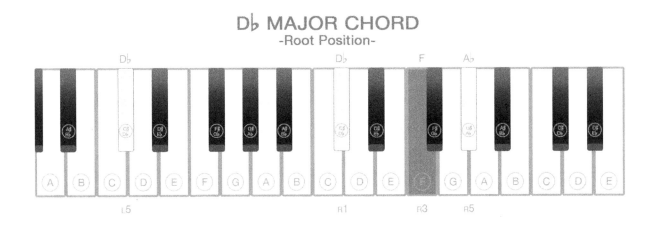

## Db MAJOR CHORD
### -Second Inversion-

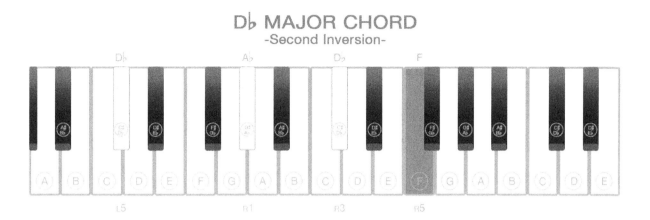

# Eb chord and its inversions

The 5 chord is Eb. You've now played an Eb chord in the keys of Bb, Eb, and Ab. The inversions are the same for all of them, so you're ahead of the game here.

## Eb MAJOR CHORD
### -Root Position-

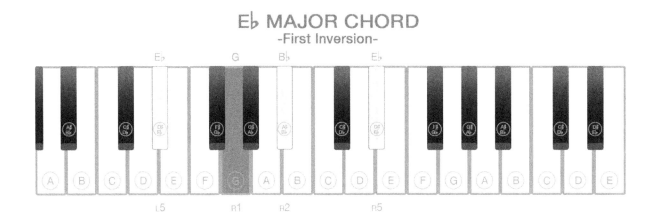

## Fm chord and its inversions

The 6m chord is Fm. An Fm and an A♭ chord are nearly the same set of notes, except that the E♭ note in an A♭ chord has been raised to an F note in the Fm. Here's how to play all three Fm chords.

## F MINOR CHORD
### -Root Position-

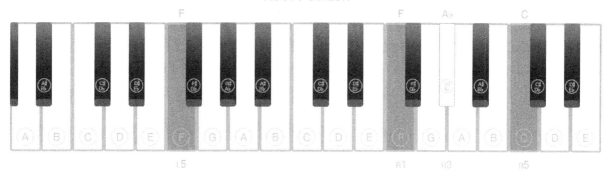

## F MINOR CHORD
### -First Inversion-

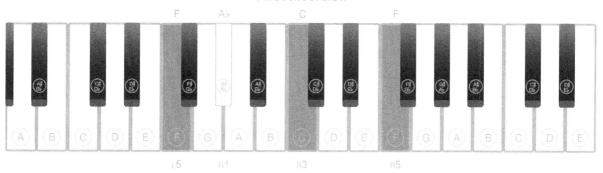

## F MINOR CHORD
### -Second Inversion-

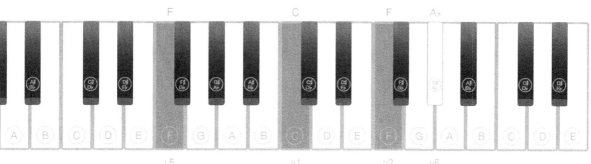

# E♭/G chord and its inversions

The 5/7 chord, or E♭/G, is the final chord for this key. The E♭/G is simple. Make sure to raise your root note from an E♭ to a G. You should experiment using other fingers on your left-hand to play the G. Perhaps use your pinky finger (L5) to play a normal E♭ chord and then switch to your middle finger (L3) to then play the G note. It should make the chord feel like it is audibly lifting upward. Here's how to play them.

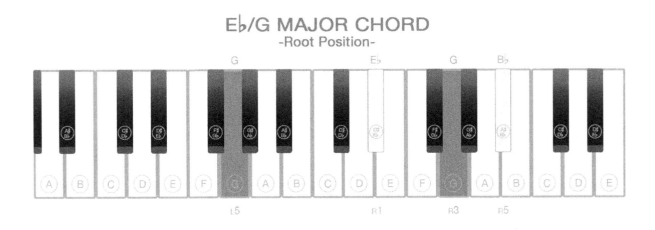

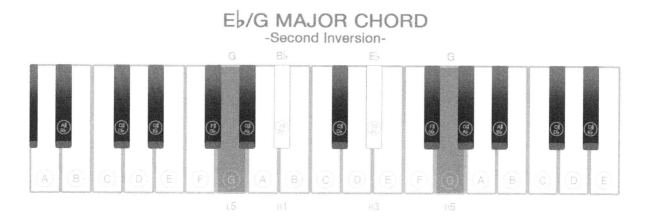

## Practice progressions

Let's try some of our practice progressions again, but using our new key of A♭. You'll need your pencils or bumpers that you used earlier. Practice will certainly make perfect in time.

### Playing chords in root position

Our first set of chords are each in root position. Your hand will be flying all over your keyboard. While it may sound beautiful, it's not efficient. We'll get into the inversions next.

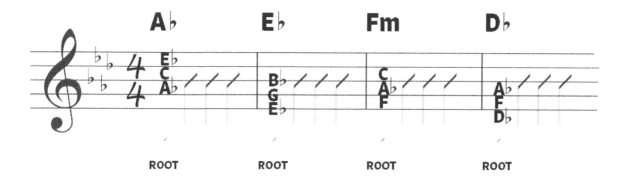

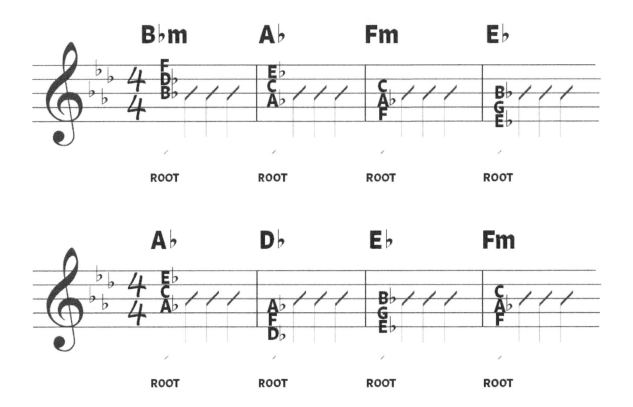

## Playing all chords between notes A♭ and G

Bring out your trusty pencils, or your bumper of choice, and place them on the G and A♭ notes. This should keep each of your chords between the A♭ and G notes. This also keeps each of your 1 chords in root position.

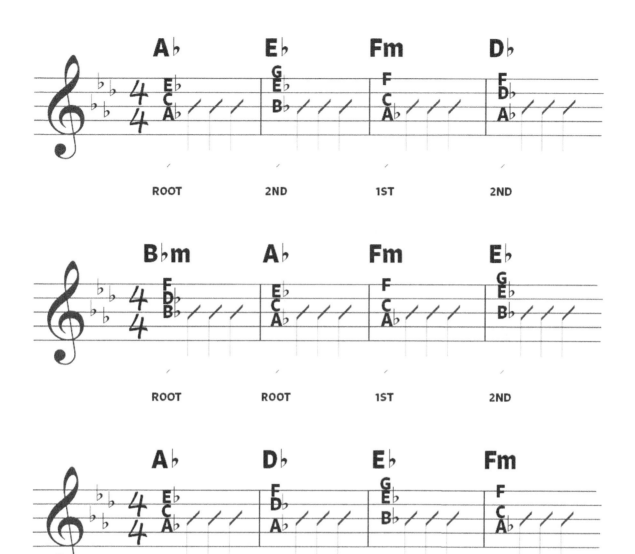

## Playing all chords between notes C and B♭

Now, move your pencils up two notes each. They should be on the notes B♭ and C. This set of inversions keeps all notes between C and B♭. This first inversion of the A♭ chord is used in each of these.

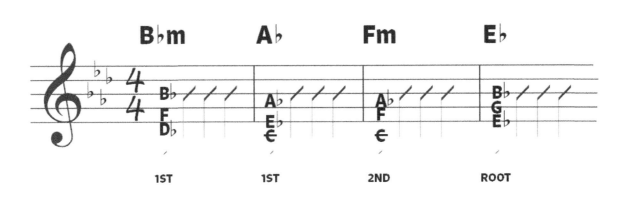

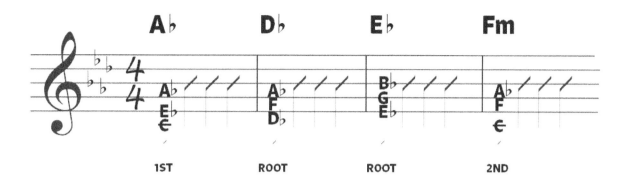

## Playing all chords between notes E♭ and D♭

Last, move your pencils up two more notes. This time you'll have pencils on D♭ and E♭. You may need to angle your pencil so that it stays on the D♭ and E♭ notes since they are raised to reach the black keys. This final set makes your A♭ chords fall into the second inversion.

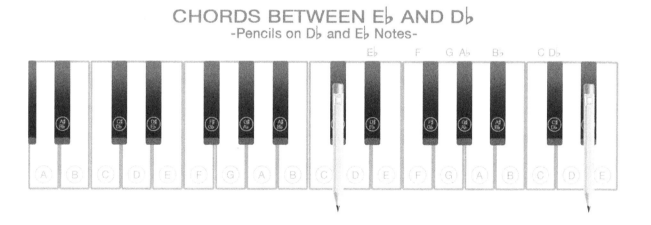

81

# The Key of D♭

## What you need to know about the key of D♭

One more tick left on the circle of fifths from the key of A♭ is the key of D♭. We will replace our G natural note with a G♭. While this key has five flat notes, I find it to be one of the easiest and most pleasant-sounding keys. Plus, it's fun to play in.

## Notes in the key of D♭ and fingering the scale

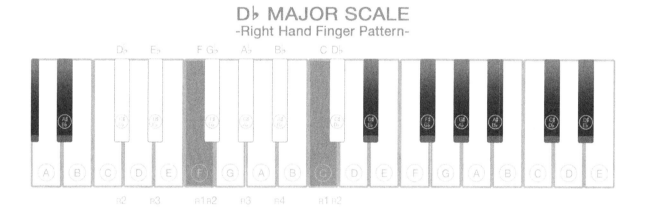

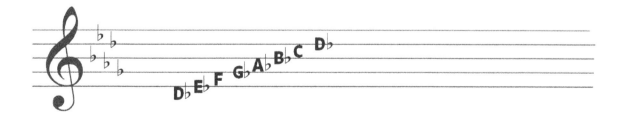

# D♭ chord and its inversions

The root chord for this key is D♭. This is the same D♭ that you used as the 4 chord in the key of A♭. Here are your fingering positions.

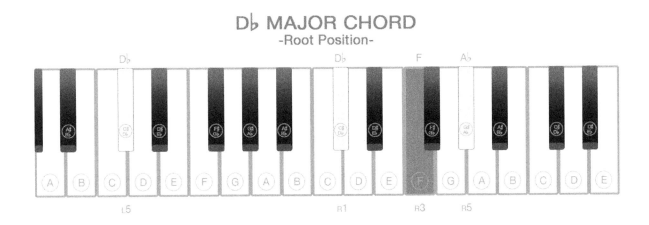

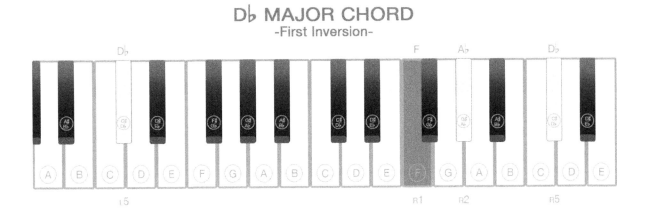

## D♭ MAJOR CHORD
### -Second Inversion-

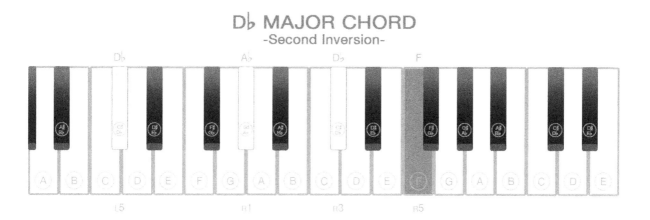

# E♭m chord and its inversions

The 2m chord is E♭m. This is the first time that you are learning this one. Take your time to get familiar with each fingering position. You'll use it in the coming chapters as well at this one.

## E♭ MINOR CHORD
### -Root Position-

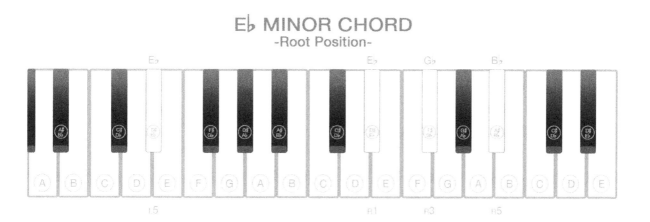

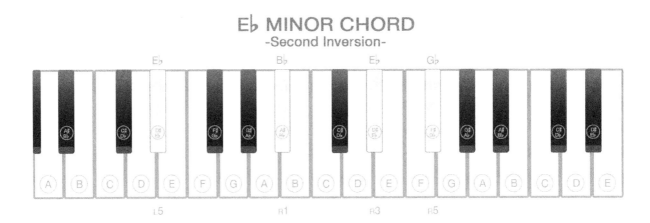

## Db/F chord and its inversions

You've already learned the Db chord. Now we'll add the F note to it to make the 1/3, or Db/F chord. Here are the positions.

## Db/F MAJOR CHORD
### -Root Position-

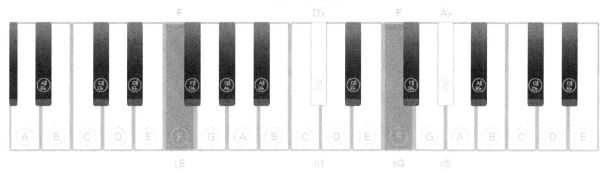

## Db/F MAJOR CHORD
### -First Inversion-

## Db/F MAJOR CHORD
### -Second Inversion-

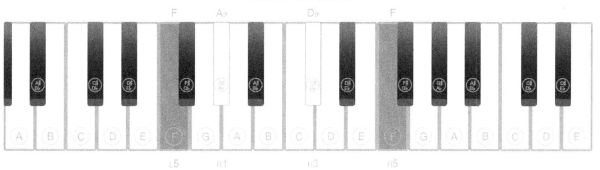

# G♭ chord and its inversions

The G♭ is the 4 chord in the key of D♭. This chord is built entirely of flat notes. While it may seem intimidating, it's actually quite playable. All three fingers are up higher on the keyboard so your fingers do not need to stretch to form this chord. All three positions are relatively easy as well. Here's how to finger a G♭.

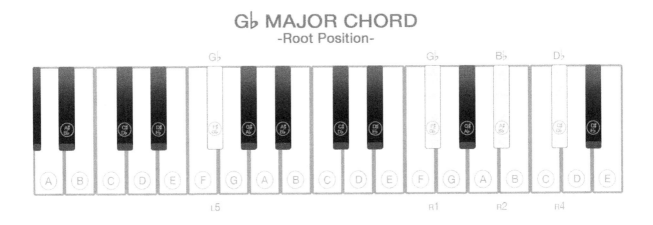

## G♭ MAJOR CHORD
### -Second Inversion-

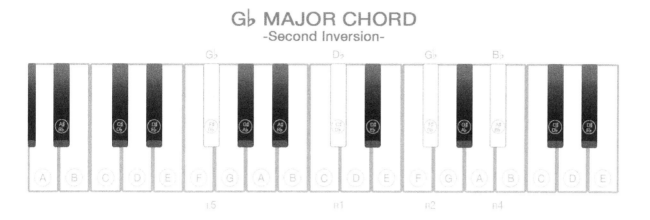

# A♭ chord and its inversions

The A♭ major chord is the 5 chord in the key of D♭. You've played this chord now three times. First in the key of E♭ (as the 4 chord), then in A♭ (as the 1 chord), and now in the key of D♭, as the 5. You should be getting used to it. Just in case you need it, here are each of the three positions for this chord. You could change around your fingering in both hands if you'd like a challenge. Try to be creative!

## A♭ MAJOR CHORD
### -Root Position-

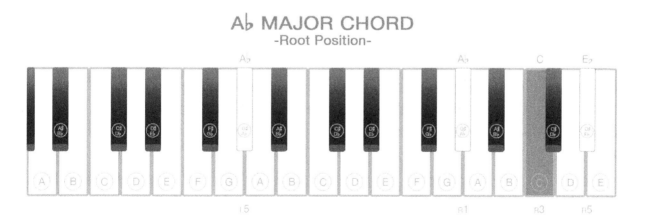

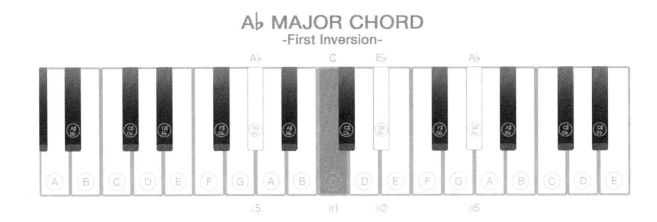

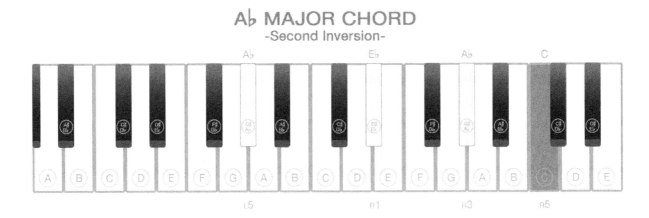

## B♭m chord and its inversions

The 6m for the key of D♭ is B♭m. The D♭ and the B♭m chords are nearly identical with the exception that the A♭ note in the D♭ chord has been moved up one to a B♭ note now in the B♭m. The left hand also moves from a D♭ to a B♭. Here is how to play each position.

## B♭ MINOR CHORD
### -Root Position-

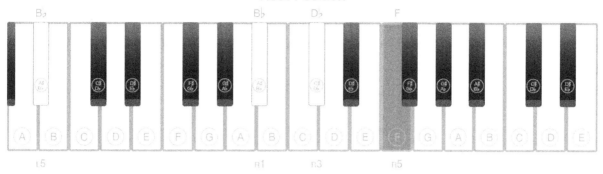

## B♭ MINOR CHORD
### -First Inversion-

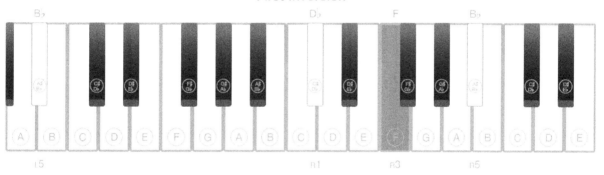

## B♭ MINOR CHORD
### -Second Inversion-

# A♭/C chord and its inversions

The A♭/C chord is the same as an A♭ chord, but the 5 note has been raised to a 7 in the left-hand. The A♭ note is now a C. Play an A♭ chord, with your pinky finger, L5, and then move to an A♭/C by using your middle finger, L3. You will lift the chord without needing to move your left-hand off the keys. Here is how to play all three positions.

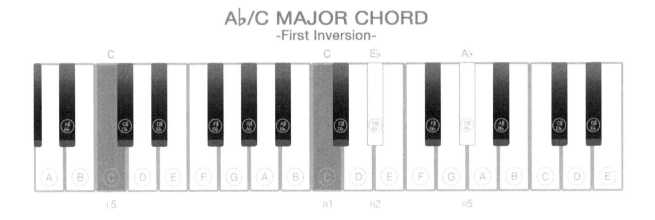

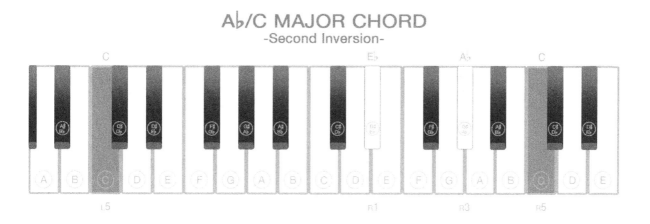

## Practice progressions

It's time for your practice progressions again. Each key that we move on to gets tougher and tougher. I recommend taking your time with each of these progressions to develop strong muscle memory.

**Playing chords in root position**

Play each of our progressions using the root position for each chord.

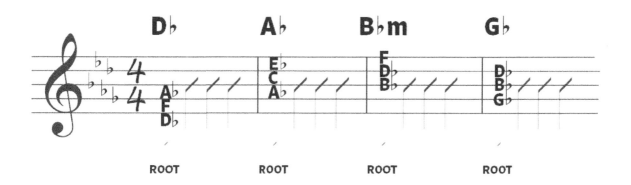

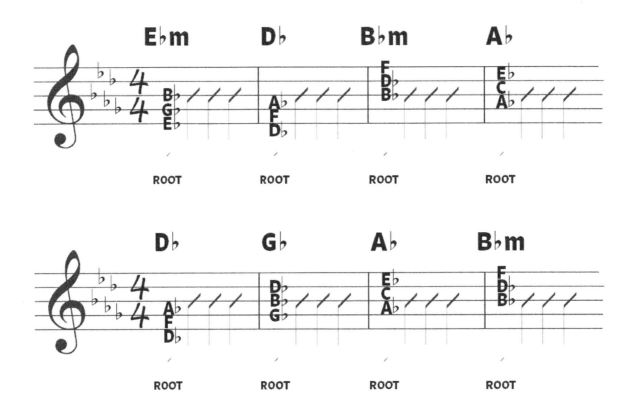

## Playing all chords between notes D♭ and C

Place your pencils on the C and D♭ notes. This should keep all of your positions between the D♭ and C notes. Notice that all of your 1 chords, D♭, will be in root position for these progressions. This means that the top note of your 1 chord is the fifth note of the D♭ scale, which is an A♭ note. This is useful when a song's melody hits an A♭ quite a bit.

# CHORDS BETWEEN D♭ AND C
## -Pencils on C and D♭ Notes-

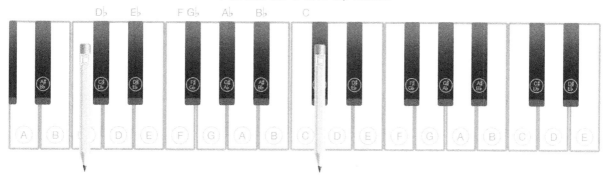

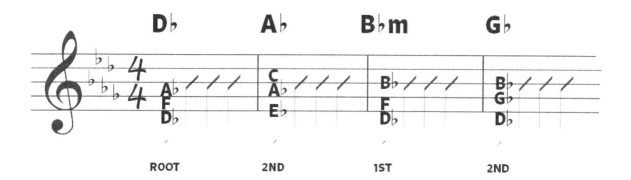

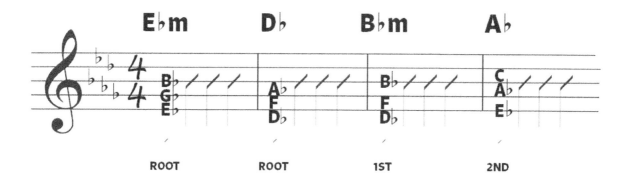

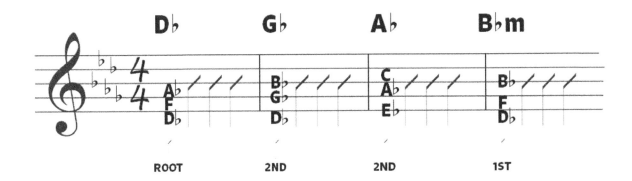

## Playing all chords between notes F and E♭

Move your pencils up two notes each. They should now rest on the E♭ and F notes. You may need to angle your pencil to let it rest on the E♭ key. All of your chords should be played between F and E♭. This places the tonic note, D♭, at the top of the D♭ chord. This is especially helpful when melodies for songs include that note quite a bit.

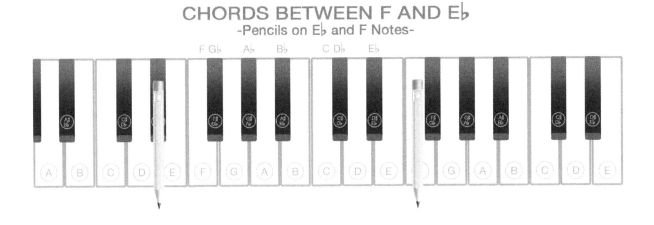

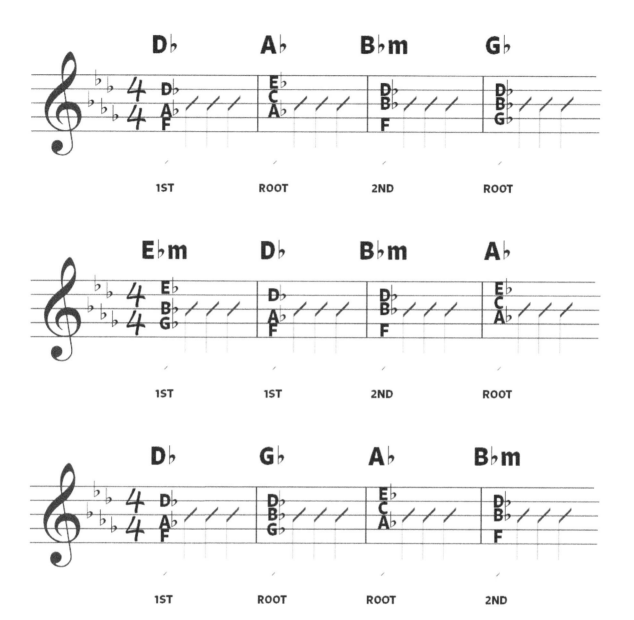

## Playing all chords between notes A♭ and G♭

Our final progressions move the pencils up two more notes. Now they should be placed on the G♭ and A♭ notes. This keeps your fingers between A♭ and G♭. The third note of the scale, F, is now on top of the D♭ chord. The third note of the scale is known as the color note, or the note which gives a chord its character.

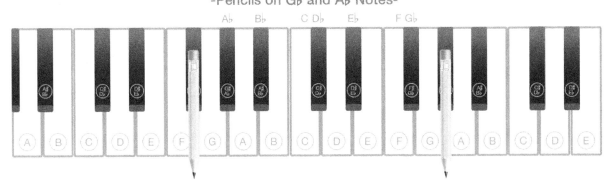

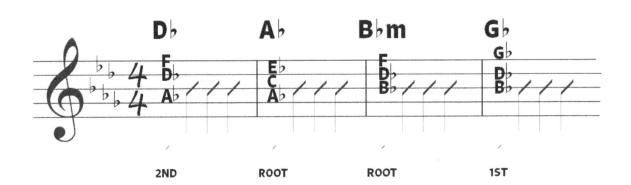

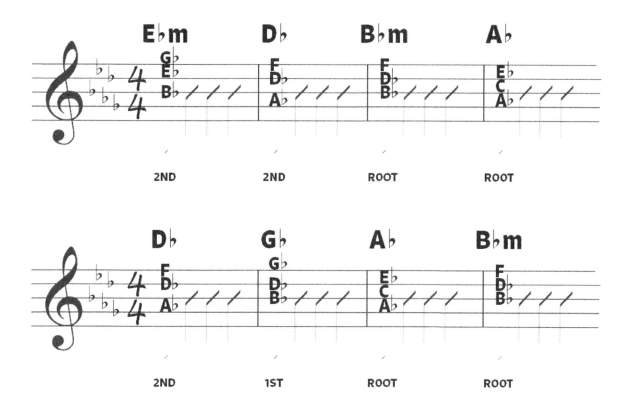

# The Key of C♯

## What you need to know about the key of C♯

If you are coming into this chapter from the previous chapter, The Key of D♭, this new key isn't going to sound any different. The key of C♯ is sonically identical to D♭, however, it is written quite different. Each of your chord names will be dropped a full letter and in most cases have their flat note replaced with a sharp. It is important to recognize that you will likely see most of the music that you buy or find online in the key of D♭, not in C♯. I only teach C♯ because guitar players tend to prefer sharps to flats, so you may see an occasional piece of music charted in this key.

## Notes in the key of C♯ and fingering the scale

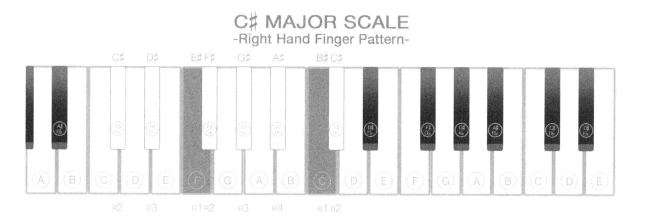

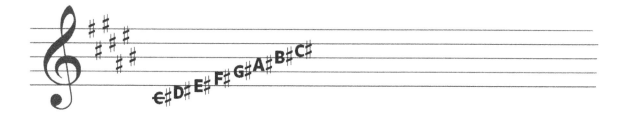

# C# chord and its inversions

The root chord for this key is C#. Remember, this is the exact same fingering as Db. I only include this as its own chapter in case you've been skipping around or would like to use this book as you would a reference manual. Here are all three positions of a C# chord.

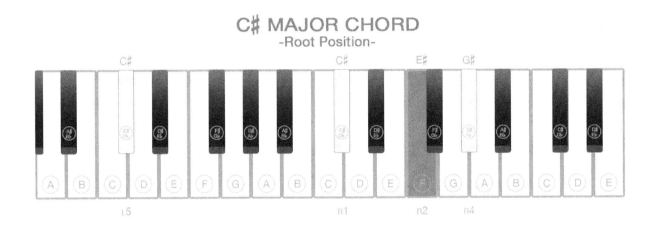

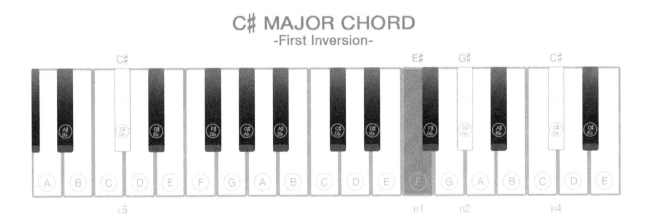

## C# MAJOR CHORD
### -Second Inversion-

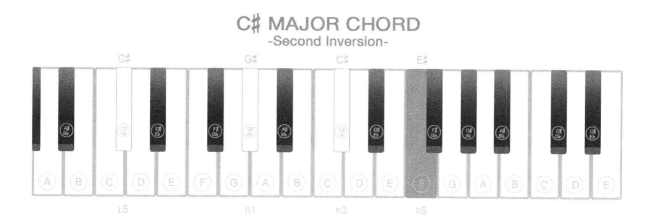

# D#m chord and its inversions

The 2m chord is D#m. This is the first time that you are learning this chord if you skipped the previous chapter. Take your time to get familiar with each fingering and position. You'll use it in the coming chapters as well at this one.

## D# MINOR CHORD
### -Root Position-

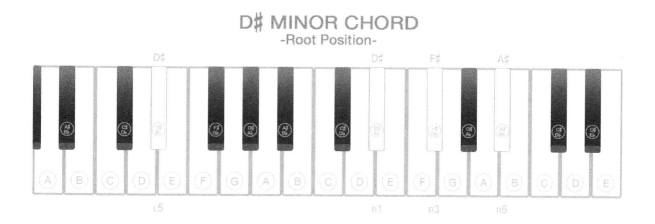

## D♯ MINOR CHORD
### -First Inversion-

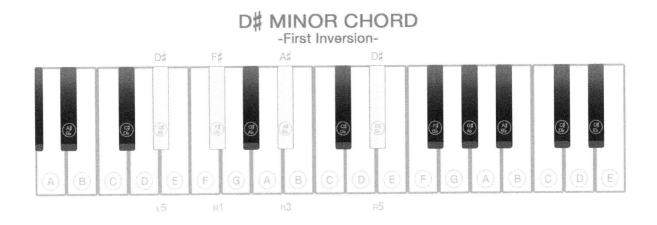

## D♯ MINOR CHORD
### -Second Inversion-

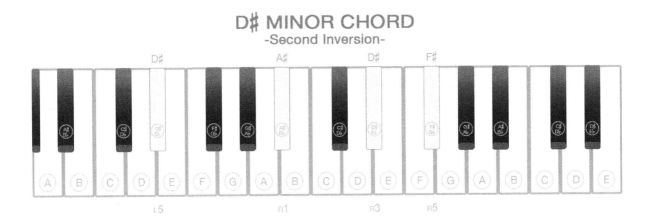

# C♯/E♯ chord and its inversions

You've already learned the C♯ chord. Now we'll replace the C♯ with the E♯ note to make the C♯/E♯ chord. It's the 1/3 in the key of C♯. Here are the positions.

## C#/E# MAJOR CHORD
### -Root Position-

## C#/E# MAJOR CHORD
### -First Inversion-

## C#/E# MAJOR CHORD
### -Second Inversion-

# F♯ chord and its inversions

The F♯ is the 4 chord in the key of C♯. This chord uses entirely sharp notes. While it may seem intimidating, it's actually quite easy. All three fingers are up higher up on the keyboard so there is far less stretching. In a few chapters, the F♯ chord will be the star of its own key. Get to know it well in this key first. Here are the three positions.

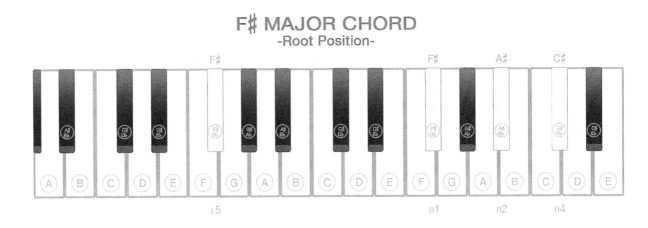

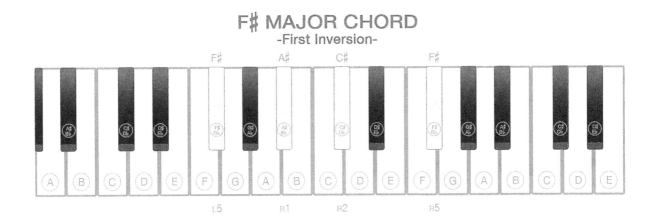

### F♯ MAJOR CHORD
#### -Second Inversion-

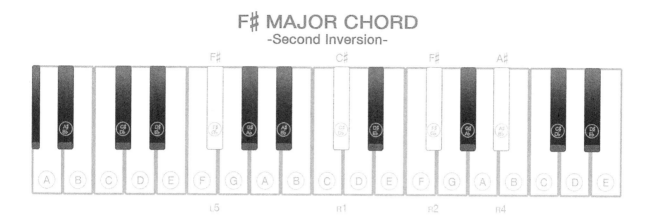

# G♯ chord and its inversions

The G♯ major chord is the 5 chord in the key of C♯. You've played this chord now three times. First in the key of E♭ (known as the A♭), then in the key of A♭, and now finally in the key of C♯. Just in case you need a refresher, here are each of the three positions for this chord. You could change around the fingerings in both hands if you'd like a challenge. Try to be creative!

### G♯ MAJOR CHORD
#### -Root Position-

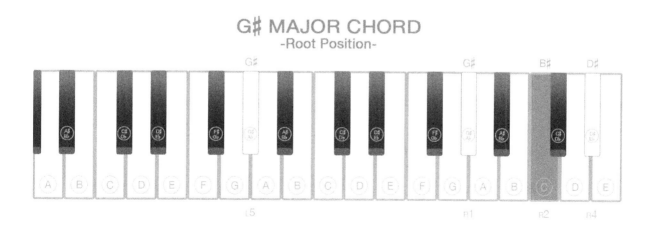

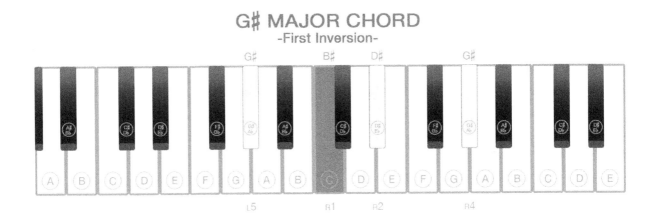

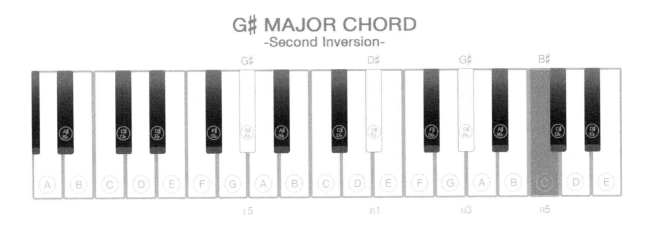

## A#m chord and its inversions

The 6m for the key of C# is A#m. The A# and the A#m are nearly identical save that the D note in the A# chord has been moved down one to the C# note now in the A#m chord. Here is how to play each position.

# A♯ MINOR CHORD
### -Root Position-

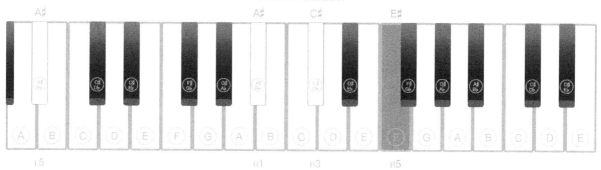

# A♯ MINOR CHORD
### -First Inversion-

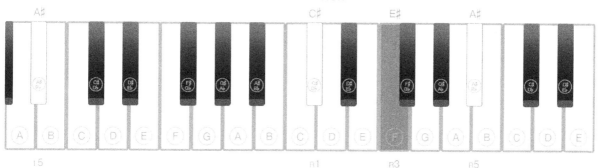

# A♯ MINOR CHORD
### -Second Inversion-

# G♯/B♯ chord and its inversions

The G♯/B♯ chord is the same as a G♯ chord, but the 5 note has been raised to a 7 in the left-hand. The G♯ note is now a B♯. Play a G♯ chord, with your pinky finger, L5, and then move to a G♯/B♯ by using your middle finger, L3. It will lift the chord without needing to move your left-hand off of the keys. Here is how to play all three positions.

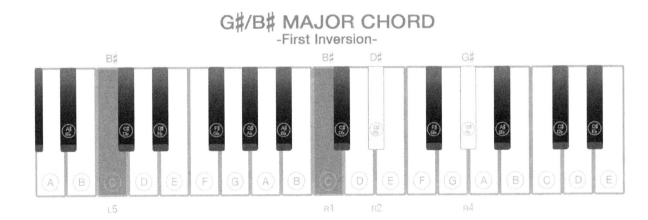

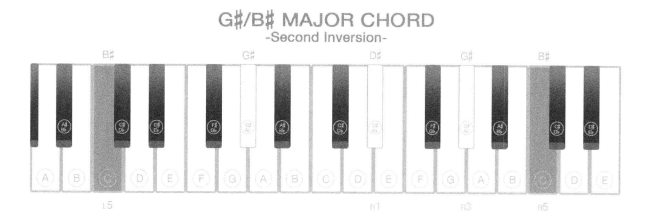

# Practice progressions

It's time for your practice progressions again. Each key that we move to gets tougher and tougher. I recommend taking your time with each of these progressions as you develop muscle memory.

**Playing chords in root position**

Play each of our progressions using the root position for each chord.

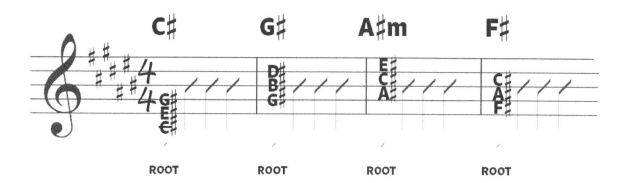

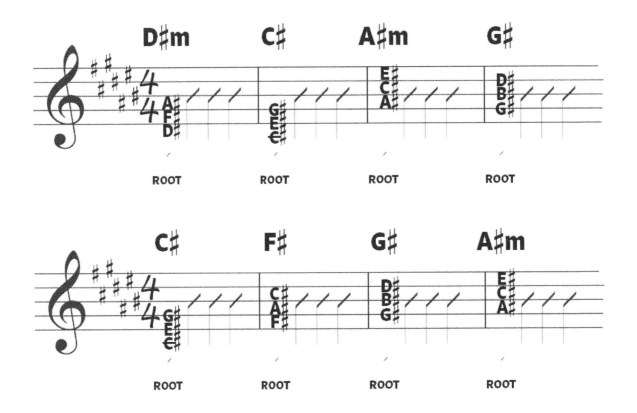

## Playing all chords between notes C♯ and B♯

Place your pencils on the B♯ and C♯ notes. This should keep all of your positions between the C♯ and B♯ notes. Notice that all of your 1 chords, C♯, will be in root position for these progressions. This means that the top note of your 1 chord is the fifth note of the C♯ scale, which is a G♯ note. This is useful when a song's melody hits a G♯ quite a bit.

# CHORDS BETWEEN C♯ AND B♯
## -Pencils on B♯ and C♯ Notes-

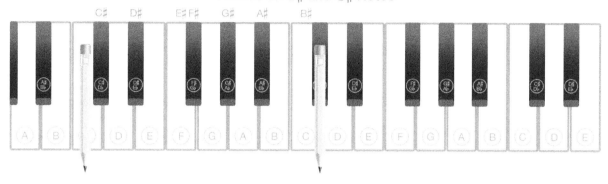

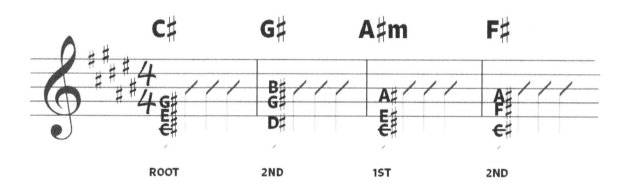

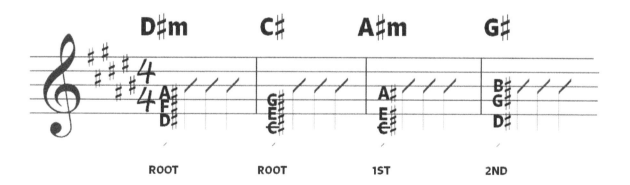

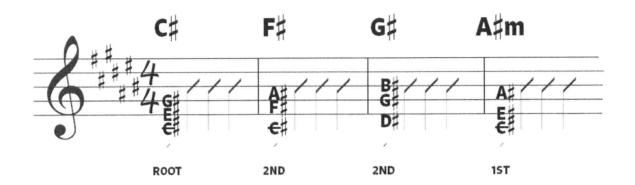

## Playing all chords between notes E♯ and D♯

Move your pencils up two notes each. They should now rest on the D♯ and E♯ notes. You may need to angle your pencil to let it rest on these keys. All of your chords should be played between E♯ and D♯. This places the tonic note, C♯, at the top of the C♯ chord. This is especially helpful when melodies for songs include that note quite a bit.

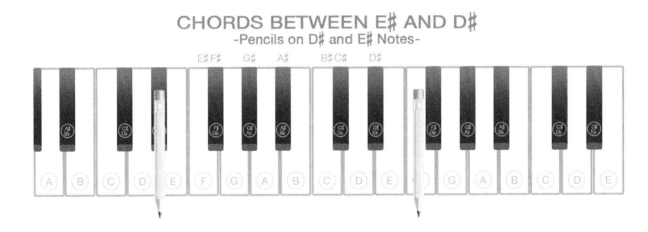

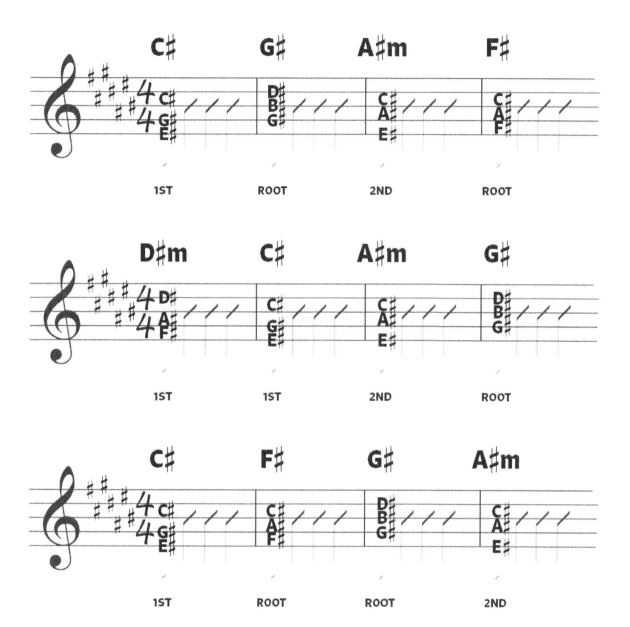

## Playing all chords between notes G♯ and F♯

Our final progressions move the pencils up two more keys. Now they should be placed on the F♯ and G♯ notes. This keeps your fingers between F♯ and G♯. The third note of the scale, E♯, is now on top of the C♯ chord. The third note of the scale is known as the color note, or the note which gives a chord its character.

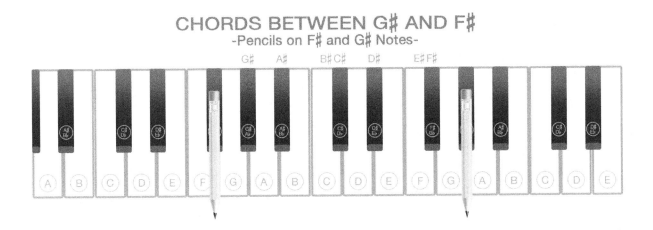

CHORDS BETWEEN G♯ AND F♯
-Pencils on F♯ and G♯ Notes-

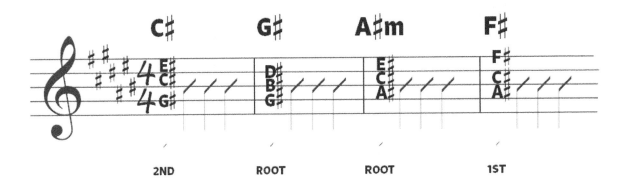

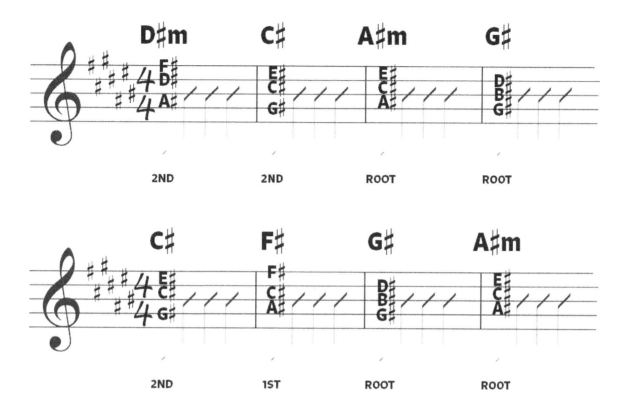

# The Key of G♭

## What you need to know about the key of G♭

One more tick left on the circle of fifths from the key of D♭ is the key of G♭. Even though you may find this key tough, you may also find it to be the sweetest and most pleasant sounding. Since each and every flat note is employed, fingering these chords–and even the scale–can prove difficult. Hopefully, that difficulty will diminish with practice. Today, after several years of practicing in this key, I enjoy playing in it. I hope you will too.

## Notes in the key of G♭ and fingering the scale

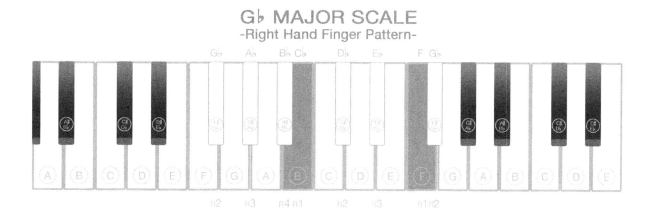

# G♭ chord and its inversions

The root chord for this key is G♭. This is the same G♭ that you used as the 4 chord in the key of D♭. The other name for this chord, as you'll see in the next chapter, is F♯. If you've worked through *Piano Chords One*, then you'll remember it as the 5 chord in the key of B. This is that same chord, but using flat notes rather than sharp. Here are your fingering positions.

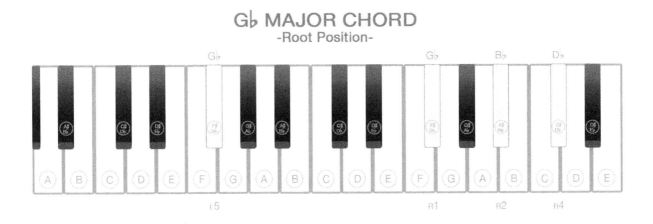

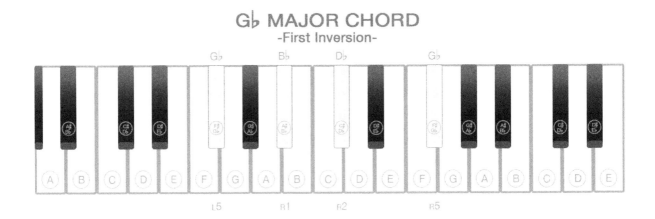

## Gb MAJOR CHORD
### -Second Inversion-

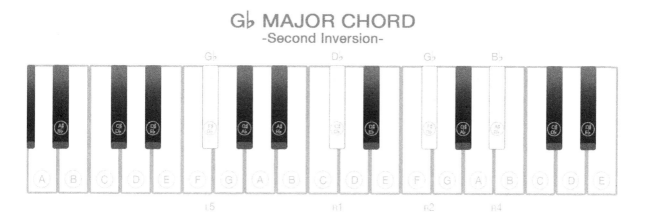

# Abm chord and its inversions

The 2m chord is Abm. This is the first time you are seeing this one. It's only a touch more difficult than its major counterpart, Ab. You will only need to move your C natural note to a Cb note. Please note that a Cb and a B are one and the same. It's one key to the left. Here are all three positions.

## Ab MINOR CHORD
### -Root Position-

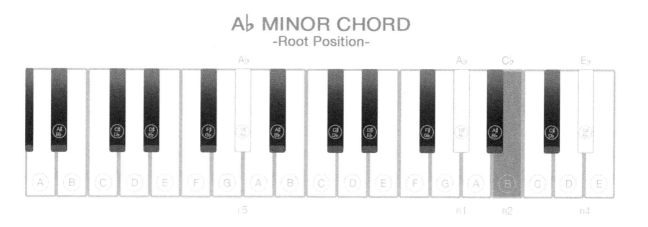

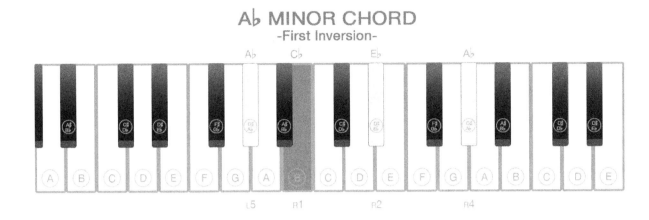

# G♭/B♭ chord and its inversions

This is the first time you are learning the G♭/B♭ chord. Since you've mastered the G♭ chord, you're in business. You need to raise the root note from a G♭ to a B♭. Here are the positions.

## Gb/Bb MAJOR CHORD
### -Root Position-

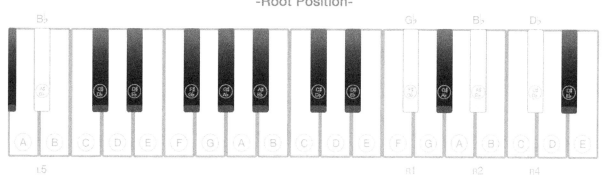

## Gb/Bb MAJOR CHORD
### -First Inversion-

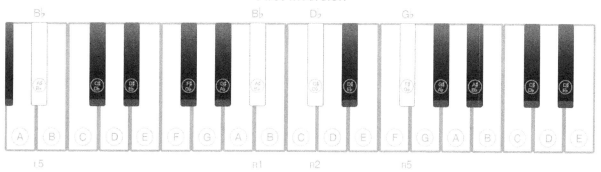

## Gb/Bb MAJOR CHORD
### -Second Inversion-

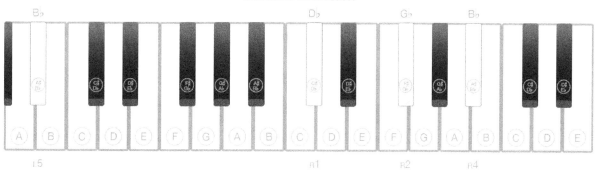

# C♭ chord and its inversions

You will rarely see a C♭ chord out in the wild–in everyday music performance. It's because it's typically called a B chord. However, if you follow proper rules for music, the B chord isn't used in the key of G♭. Instead, you'll find the C♭. The reason makes sense: There is already a B♭ in this key, so also including a B natural would mean there are two notes sharing the same first letter note name–thus we have the more uncommon C♭. If you're already familiar with how to play the three positions of a B chord, then you're set for C♭. They are exactly the same. However, if you haven't played either yet, this is how to finger each position.

## C♭ MAJOR CHORD
### -Root Position-

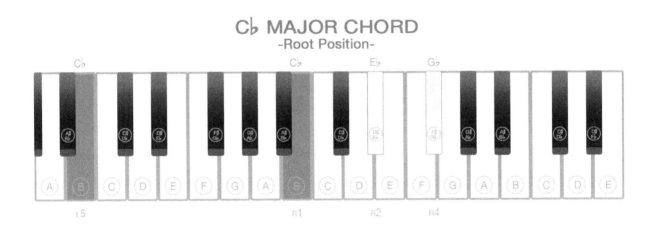

## C♭ MAJOR CHORD
### -First Inversion-

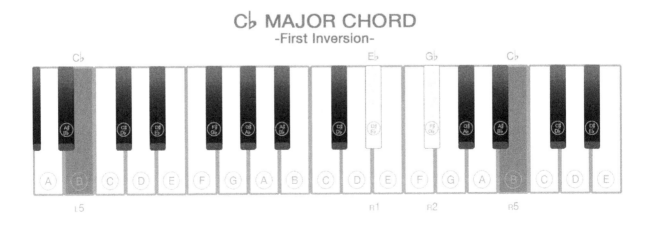

## C♭ MAJOR CHORD
### -Second Inversion-

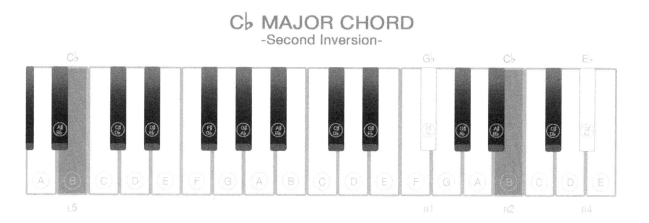

# D♭ chord and its inversions

The D♭ major chord is the 5 chord in the key of G♭. This is the third time you are playing through this one. It was the 4 chord in the key of A♭, the 1 chord in the key of D♭, and now the 5 in the key of G♭. Here are all three positions.

## D♭ MAJOR CHORD
### -Root Position-

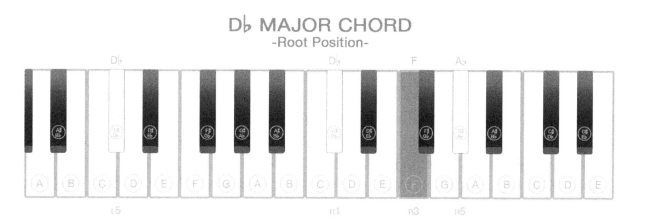

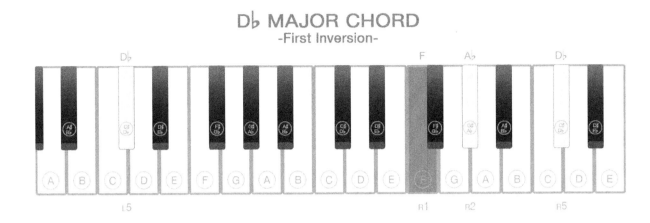

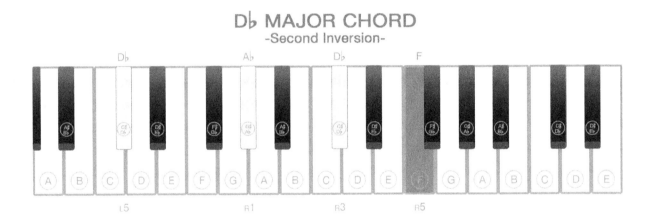

# E♭m chord and its inversions

The 6m for the key of G♭ is E♭m. Like several chords before, this is the first time that we are playing this one. If there is an upside to this one it's that an E♭m is slightly easier to play when compared to its major chord counterpart. While playing an E♭, you must include one natural note (white key). On the other hand, the E♭m chord is played solely using flat notes (black keys). Here is how to play all three positions of an E♭m.

## Eb MINOR CHORD
### -Root Position-

## Eb MINOR CHORD
### -First Inversion-

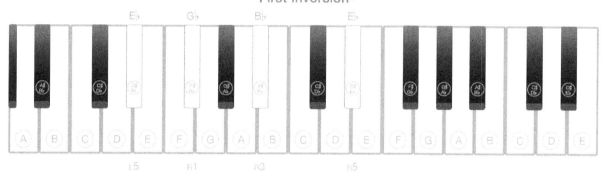

## Eb MINOR CHORD
### -Second Inversion-

# D♭/F chord and its inversions

The D♭/F chord is the same as a D♭ chord, only the 5th note of the G♭ scale, D♭, has been raised to a 7 in the left-hand. The D♭ note is now an F natural for the left-hand. Here is how to play all three positions.

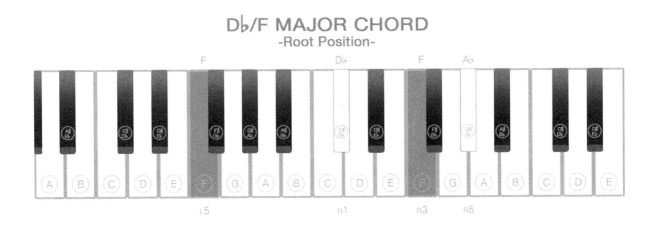

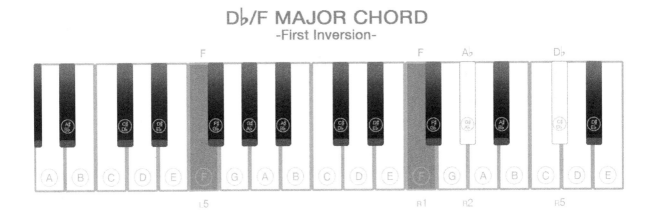

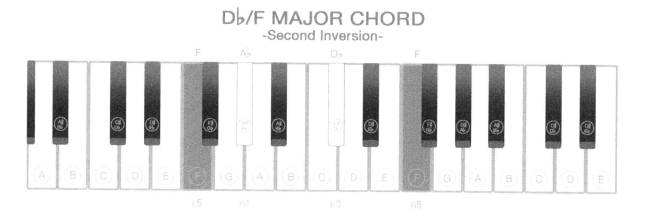

## Practice progressions

It's time for your practice progressions again. Each key that we move to gets tougher and tougher. I recommend taking your time with each of these progressions as you develop muscle memory.

**Playing chords in root position**

Play each of your progressions using the root position for each chord.

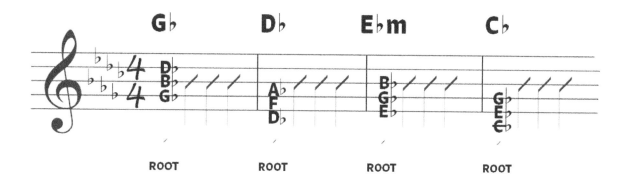

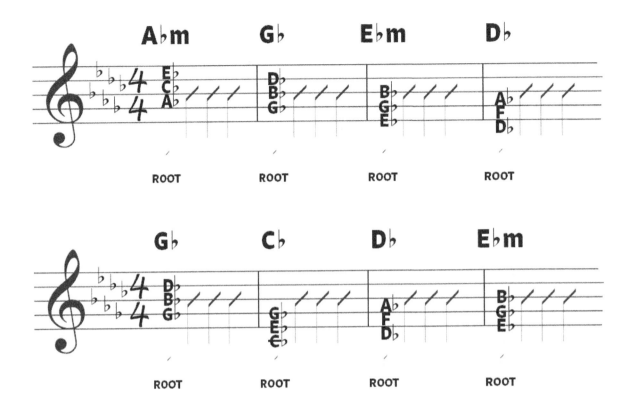

## Playing all chords between notes G♭ and F

Place your pencils on the F and G♭ notes. This should keep all of your positions between the G♭ and F notes. Notice that all of your 1 chords, G♭, will be in root position for these progressions. This means that the top note of your 1 chord is the fifth note of the G♭ scale, which is a D♭ note. This is useful when a song's melody hits a D♭ quite a bit.

## CHORDS BETWEEN G♭ AND F
### -Pencils on F and G♭ Notes-

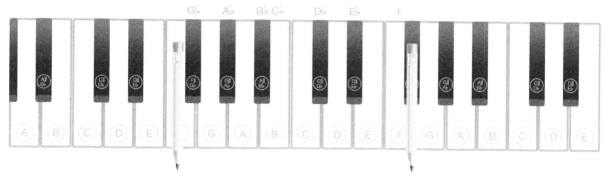

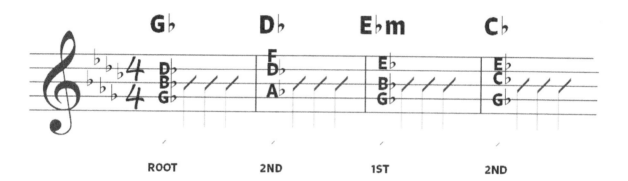

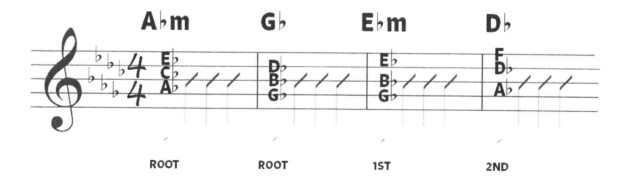

131

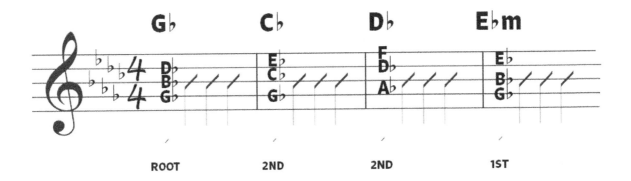

**Playing all chords between notes B♭ and A♭**

Move your pencils up two notes each. They should now rest on the A♭ and B♭ notes. You may need to angle your pencil to let it rest on the black keys. All of your chords should be played between B♭ and A♭. This places the tonic note, G♭, at the top of the G♭ chord. This is especially helpful when melodies for songs include that note quite a bit.

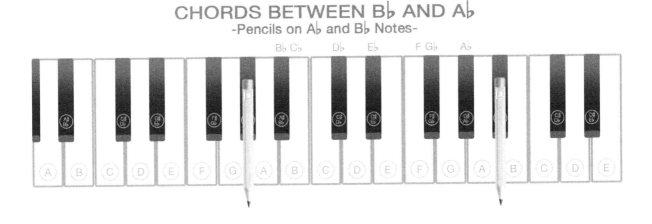

CHORDS BETWEEN B♭ AND A♭
-Pencils on A♭ and B♭ Notes-

## Playing all chords between notes D♭ and C♭

Our final progressions move the pencils up two more keys. Now they should be placed on the C♭ and D♭ notes. This keeps your fingers between D♭ and C♭. The third note of the scale, B♭, is now on top of the G♭ chord. The third note of the scale is known as the color note, or the note which gives a chord its character.

CHORDS BETWEEN D♭ AND C♭
-Pencils on C♭ and D♭ Notes-

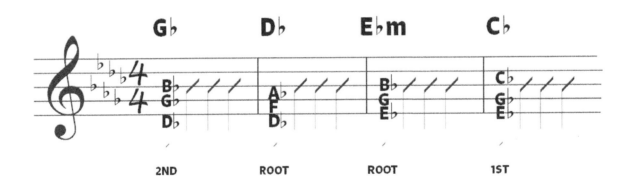

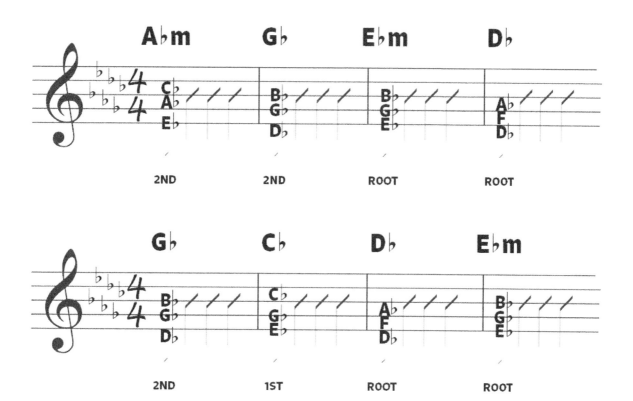

# The Key of F♯

## What you need to know about the key of F♯

As I mentioned in the chapter concerning the key of C♯, you're likely coming to this chapter from the previous one, The Key of G♭. F♯ isn't going to sound any different to you than the previous key. While the key of F♯ is sonically identical to G♭, it is written very differently. Each of your chord names will be dropped a full letter name and in most cases have their flats replaced with sharps. It is important to note that you will likely see most sheet music that you purchase in the key of G♭ and not in F♯. I only teach the key of F♯ because guitar players tend to prefer sharps to flats, so you will see an occasional piece of written music charted this way.

## Notes in the key of F♯ and fingering the scale

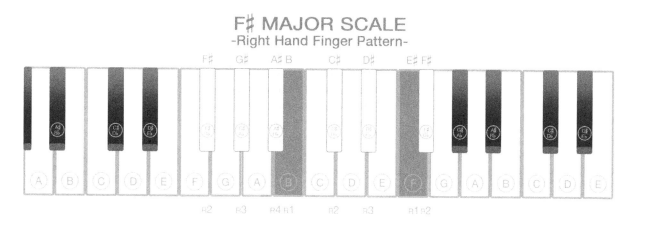

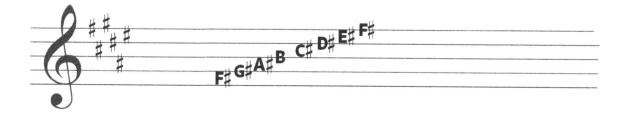

# F♯ chord and its inversions

The root chord for this key is F♯. This is the same F♯ that you used as the 4 chord in the key of C♯. It is also the 5 chord in the key of B, which is found in the last chapter of the previous book in this series, *Piano Chords One*. Here are the finger positions.

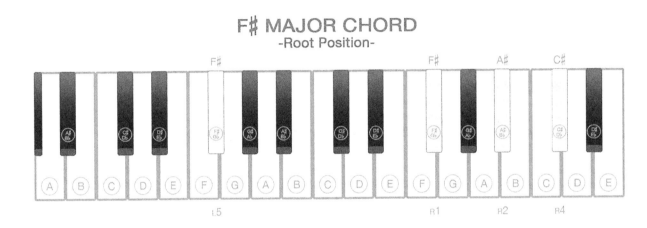

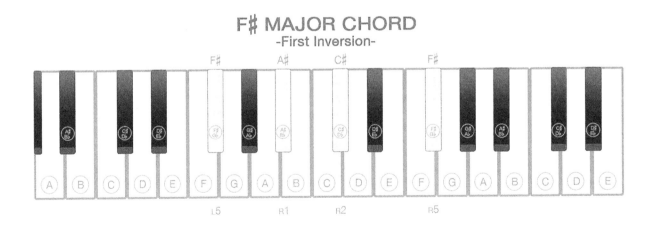

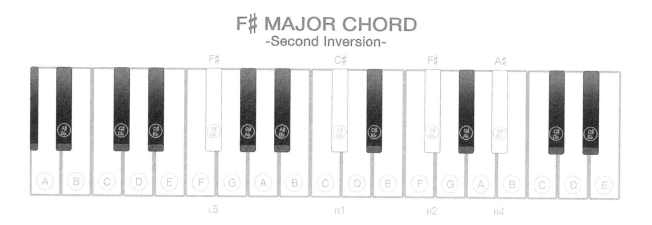

**F♯ MAJOR CHORD**
-Second Inversion-

## G♯m chord and its inversions

The 2m chord is G♯m. This is the first time you are seeing this one. It's only a touch more difficult than its major counterpart, G♯. You will only need to move your C natural note to a B note. It's one small move left. Here are all three positions.

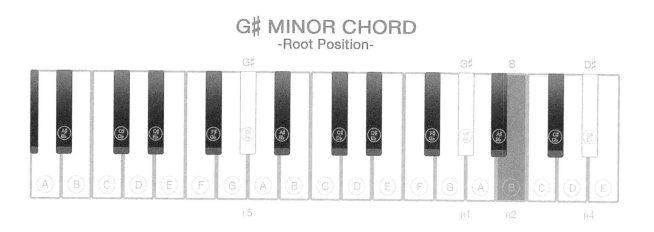

**G♯ MINOR CHORD**
-Root Position-

## G♯ MINOR CHORD
### -First Inversion-

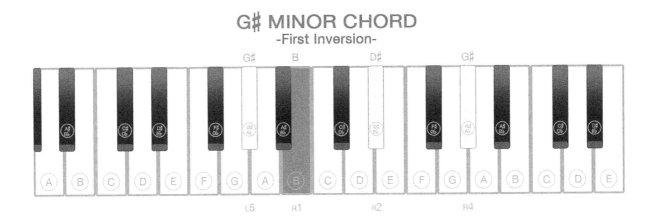

## G♯ MINOR CHORD
### -Second Inversion-

# F♯/A♯ chord and its inversions

This is the first time you are learning the F♯/A♯ chord as well. It's the 1/3 chord in this key. If you've mastered the F♯ chord, then you're in business. You only need to raise the root note from an F♯ to an A♯. Here are the positions.

## F#/A# MAJOR CHORD
### -Root Position-

## F#/A# MAJOR CHORD
### -First Inversion-

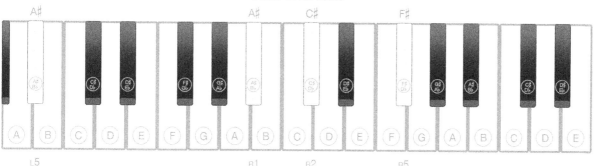

## F#/A# MAJOR CHORD
### -Second Inversion-

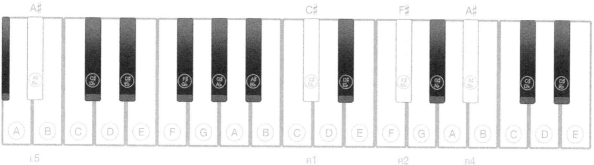

# B chord and its inversions

If you finished my first book, *Piano Chords One*, then you'll remember playing the B chord often. In fact, The Key of B was the final chapter of that book. In this case, you'd have played this chord several times. As we saw from the previous chapter, G♭, this chord also has the name C♭, however, it's extremely rare to see B named C♭ unless you are reading classical sheet music. Here are each of the finger positions for B.

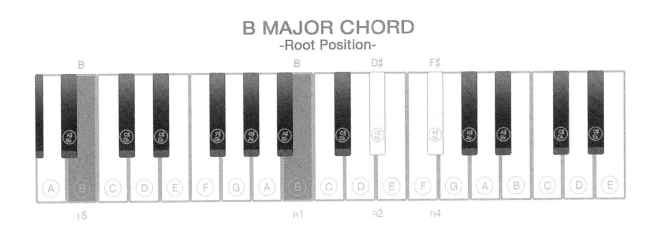

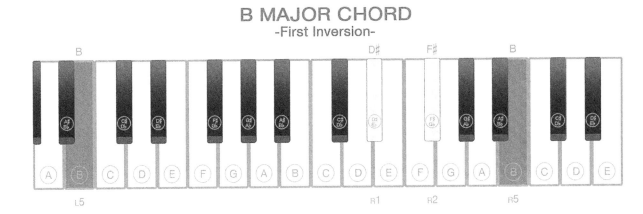

## B MAJOR CHORD
### -Second Inversion-

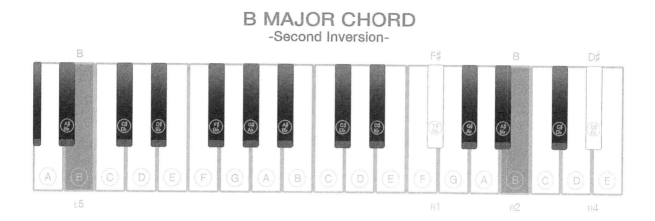

# C♯ chord and its inversions

The C♯ major chord is the 5 chord in the key of F♯. This is the third time you are playing through this one. It was the 4 chord in the key of A♭ (known as the G♯ chord); the 1 chord in the key of C♯ (also known as the key of D♭), and now the 5 in the key of F♯. Here is each position.

## C♯ MAJOR CHORD
### -Root Position-

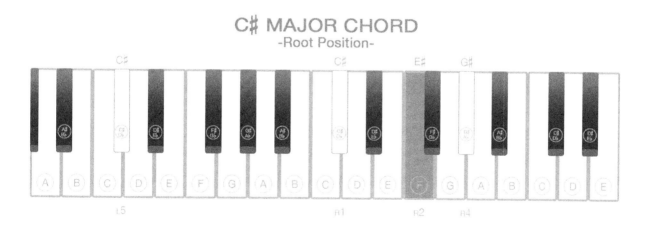

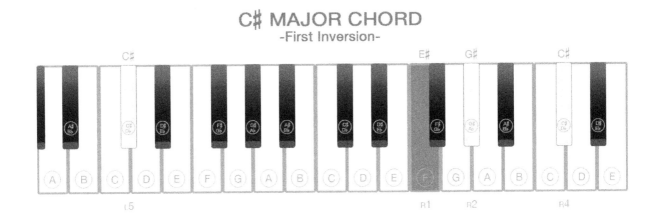

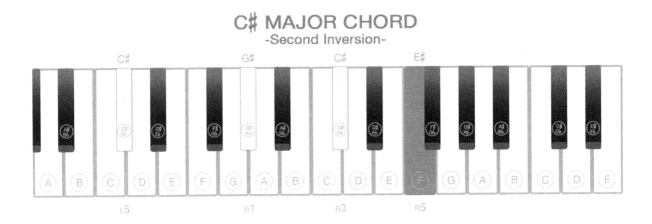

## D#m chord and its inversions

The 6m for the key of F# is D#m. If there is an upside to this one it's that a D#m is slightly easier to play as compared to its major chord counterpart. While playing a D#, you must include one natural (white key). The D#m is played solely using sharp notes (black keys). Remember, this chord is also known as E♭m. Here's how to play all three positions.

## D# MINOR CHORD
### -Root Position-

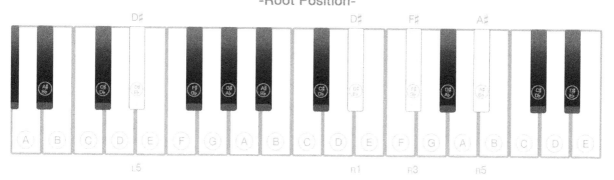

## D# MINOR CHORD
### -First Inversion-

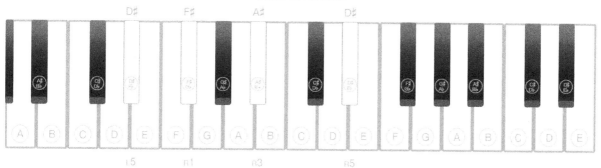

## D# MINOR CHORD
### -Second Inversion-

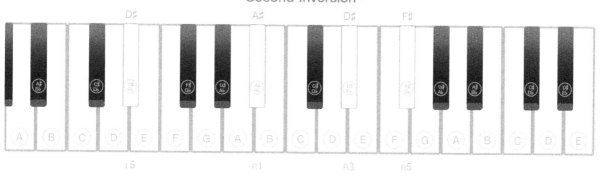

# C#/E# chord and its inversions

The C#/E# chord is the same as a C#, but the root note has been raised up two in the left-hand. The C# note is now an E#. Here is how to play all three positions.

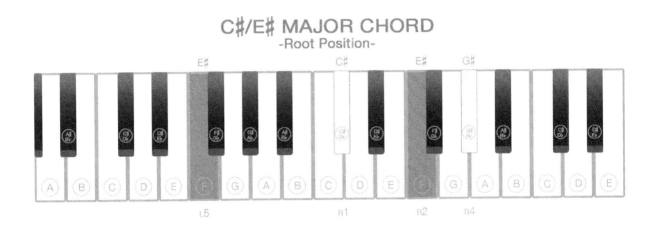

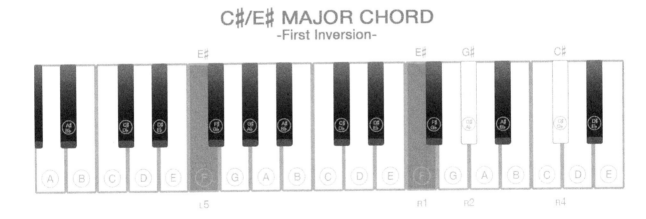

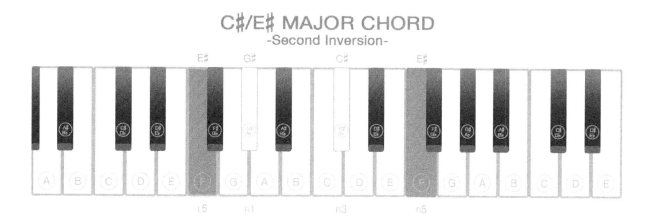

## Practice progressions

It's time for your practice progressions again. Each key that we move to gets tougher and tougher. I recommend taking your time with each of these progressions as you develop muscle memory.

**Playing chords in root position**

Play each of our progressions using the root position for each chord.

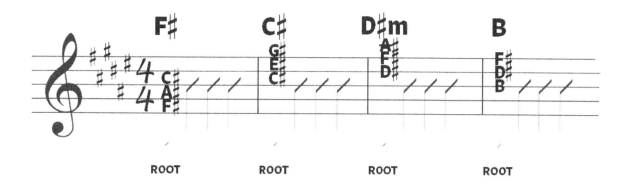

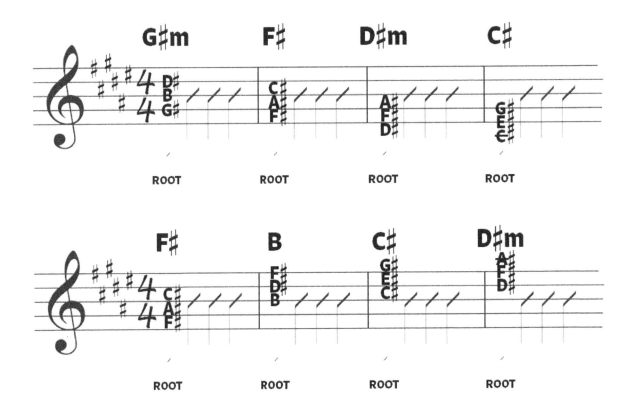

## Playing all chords between notes F♯ and E♯

Place your pencils on the E♯ and F♯ notes. This should keep all of your positions between the F♯ and E♯ notes. Notice that all of your 1 chords, F♯, will be in root position for these progressions. This means that the top note of your 1 chord is the fifth note of the F♯ scale, which is a C♯ note. This is useful when a song's melody hits a C♯ quite a bit.

## CHORDS BETWEEN F♯ AND E♯
### -Pencils on E♯ and F♯ Notes-

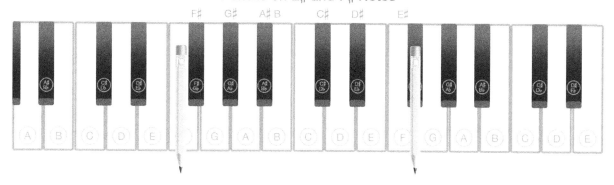

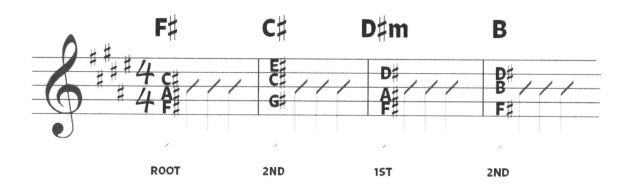

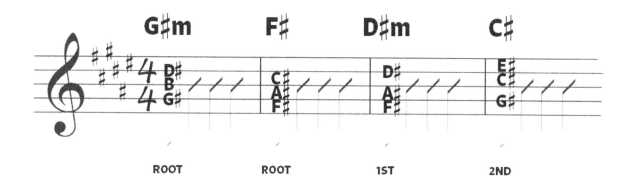

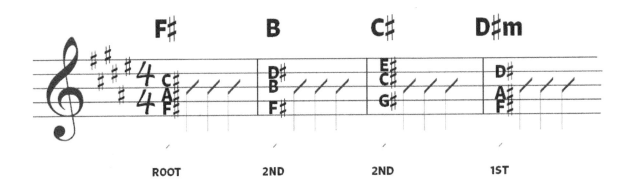

## Playing all chords between notes A♯ and G♯

Move your pencils up two notes each. They should now rest on the G♯ and A♯ notes. All of your chords should be played between A♯ and G♯. This places the tonic note, F♯, at the top of the F♯ chord. This is especially helpful when melodies for songs include that note quite a bit.

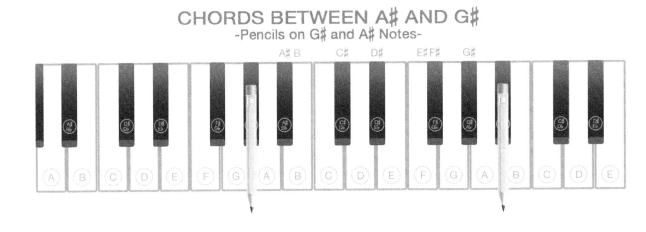

CHORDS BETWEEN A♯ AND G♯
-Pencils on G♯ and A♯ Notes-

## Playing all chords between notes C♯ and B

Our final progressions move the pencils up two more keys. Now they should be placed on the B and C♯ notes. This keeps your fingers between C♯ and B. The third note of the scale, A♯, is now on top of the F♯ chord. The third note of the scale is known as the color note, or the note which gives a chord its character.

CHORDS BETWEEN C♯ AND B
-Pencils on B and C♯ Notes-

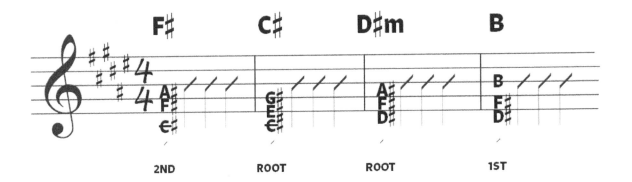

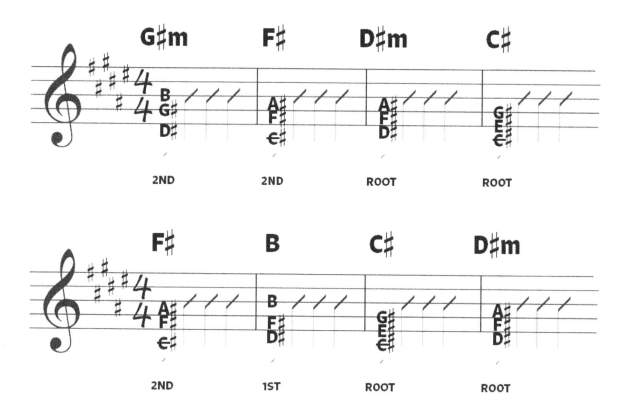

# Conclusion

## You've just crossed the finish line!

You've done it! You've made it all the way from the key of B♭ to the key of F♯. This is huge! We have covered quite a bit of material! You should now be able to look over the chords for some of your favorite songs and be able to play them! It wouldn't matter if the song was in the key of C♯ or A♭, you know how to play in any of the flat keys now. This is quite a feat!

So, what about some real songs to play? Here's an answer to your important question. You have played three progressions in seven different keys throughout this book. Did you know that these progressions are the backbones for some of the most famous songs? Even if you don't like the artists below, it's cool to know that you now know how to play their music. For instance, look at this list of famous songs that use our first progression.

**Songs using our 1, 5, 6m, 4 progression:**

Let It Be (The Beatles)
Auld Lang Syne (Traditional New Year Song)
Let It Go (The Movie *Frozen*)
Innocent (Taylor Swift)
Don't Stop Believin' (Journey)

## Fakebooks, the internet, and something called "guitar chords"

I'm betting that you'd love some resources to help you learn some songs. After all, we now have an arsenal of chords with which to use. Here are three that I recommend with which you become familiar. They are fakebooks, the internet, and something called *guitar chords*.

Fakebooks are better known as lead sheets but were coined *fakebooks* several years ago. A lead sheet has chords written on top of a melody line. While you have to do some work to figure out when to play each chord, they are succinct ways of fitting an entire song into two or three pages. You can purchase fake books on Amazon.com or wherever sheet music is typically sold in your area.

Another resource is the internet. The internet is filled with vast amounts of written music that you can play. There is a wide spectrum of quality content too. You could buy professionally transcribed full scores (where every note is written out) all the way to *Back-Woods-Johnny's version of a song he transcribed in his basement*. A quick search using the term "[song title] sheet music" should produce several ways to play the song you're looking for.

You could also search for the term "[song title] guitar chords". While it's true that you're looking to play the song on the piano, using the search term "guitar chords" should yield everything you need to play the song. A guitar chord chart, or just a *chord chart*, includes the chords written atop the lyrics. This is also a succinct way to transcribe a song. It's critical to mention that *Johnny in his basement* may be able to publish some chord charts on his webpage, but the chords may not always be correct. These are his best guess as to what the chords should be. As a beginner/intermediate player, you should consider purchasing your sheet music, lead sheets, or chord charts. Then, you'll know that the chords are correct. Plus, you'll know that the writers of the music are being properly compensated.

# Appendix

## The bonus section

Use the following major scale fingering diagrams to learn how to play octave (eight note) scales for all major keys. This book covers the last seven of these keys: B♭, E♭, A♭, D♭, C♯, D♭, F♯, and G♭. The other keys are just as important and the material of the prior book in this series. These keys include C, G, F, D, A, E, and B.

## Major Scale Fingerings

**C Major Scale**

|  | 1 | 2 | 3 | 4 | 5 | 6 | 7 | 8 |
|---|---|---|---|---|---|---|---|---|
|  | C | D | E | F | G | A | B | C |
| Right | 1 | 2 | 3 | 1 | 2 | 3 | 4 | 5 |
| Left | 5 | 4 | 3 | 2 | 1 | 3 | 2 | 1 |

**G Major Scale**

|  | 1 | 2 | 3 | 4 | 5 | 6 | 7 | 8 |
|---|---|---|---|---|---|---|---|---|
|  | G | A | B | C | D | E | F♯ | G |
| Right | 1 | 2 | 3 | 1 | 2 | 3 | 4 | 5 |
| Left | 5 | 4 | 3 | 2 | 1 | 3 | 2 | 1 |

**F Major Scale**

|  | 1 | 2 | 3 | 4 | 5 | 6 | 7 | 8 |
|---|---|---|---|---|---|---|---|---|
|  | F | G | A | B♭ | C | D | E | F |
| Right | 1 | 2 | 3 | 4 | 1 | 2 | 3 | 4 |
| Left | 5 | 4 | 3 | 2 | 1 | 3 | 2 | 1 |

**D Major Scale**

|  | 1 | 2 | 3 | 4 | 5 | 6 | 7 | 8 |
|---|---|---|---|---|---|---|---|---|
|  | D | E | F♯ | G | A | B | C♯ | D |
| Right | 1 | 2 | 3 | 1 | 2 | 3 | 4 | 5 |
| Left | 5 | 4 | 3 | 2 | 1 | 3 | 2 | 1 |

**A Major Scale**

|  | 1 | 2 | 3 | 4 | 5 | 6 | 7 | 8 |
|---|---|---|---|---|---|---|---|---|
|  | A | B | C♯ | D | E | F♯ | G♯ | A |
| Right | 1 | 2 | 3 | 1 | 2 | 3 | 4 | 5 |
| Left | 5 | 4 | 3 | 2 | 1 | 3 | 2 | 1 |

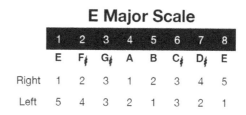

**E Major Scale**

|  | 1 | 2 | 3 | 4 | 5 | 6 | 7 | 8 |
|---|---|---|---|---|---|---|---|---|
|  | E | F♯ | G♯ | A | B | C♯ | D♯ | E |
| Right | 1 | 2 | 3 | 1 | 2 | 3 | 4 | 5 |
| Left | 5 | 4 | 3 | 2 | 1 | 3 | 2 | 1 |

## B Major Scale

|  | 1 | 2 | 3 | 4 | 5 | 6 | 7 | 8 |
|---|---|---|---|---|---|---|---|---|
|  | B | C♯ | D♯ | E | F♯ | G♯ | A♯ | B |
| Right | 1 | 2 | 3 | 1 | 2 | 3 | 4 | 5 |
| Left | 4 | 3 | 2 | 1 | 4 | 3 | 2 | 1 |

## B♭ Major Scale

|  | 1 | 2 | 3 | 4 | 5 | 6 | 7 | 8 |
|---|---|---|---|---|---|---|---|---|
|  | B♭ | C | D | E♭ | F | G | A | B♭ |
| Right | 2 | 1 | 2 | 3 | 1 | 2 | 3 | 4 |
| Left | 3 | 2 | 1 | 4 | 3 | 2 | 1 | 3 |

## E♭ Major Scale

|  | 1 | 2 | 3 | 4 | 5 | 6 | 7 | 8 |
|---|---|---|---|---|---|---|---|---|
|  | E♭ | F | G | A♭ | B♭ | C | D | E♭ |
| Right | 3 | 1 | 2 | 3 | 4 | 1 | 2 | 3 |
| Left | 3 | 2 | 1 | 4 | 3 | 2 | 1 | 3 |

## A♭ Major Scale

|  | 1 | 2 | 3 | 4 | 5 | 6 | 7 | 8 |
|---|---|---|---|---|---|---|---|---|
|  | A♭ | B♭ | C | D♭ | E♭ | F | G | A♭ |
| Right | 3 | 4 | 1 | 2 | 3 | 1 | 2 | 3 |
| Left | 3 | 2 | 1 | 4 | 3 | 2 | 1 | 3 |

## C♯/D♭ Major Scale

|  | 1 | 2 | 3 | 4 | 5 | 6 | 7 | 8 |
|---|---|---|---|---|---|---|---|---|
|  | C♯ | D♯ | E♯ | F♯ | G♯ | A♯ | B♯ | C♯ |
| Right | 2 | 3 | 1 | 2 | 3 | 4 | 1 | 2 |
| Left | 3 | 2 | 1 | 4 | 3 | 2 | 1 | 3 |

## C♯/D♭ Major Scale

|  | 1 | 2 | 3 | 4 | 5 | 6 | 7 | 8 |
|---|---|---|---|---|---|---|---|---|
|  | D♭ | E♭ | F | G♭ | A♭ | B♭ | C | D♭ |
| Right | 2 | 3 | 1 | 2 | 3 | 4 | 1 | 2 |
| Left | 3 | 2 | 1 | 4 | 3 | 2 | 1 | 3 |

## F♯/G♭ Major Scale

|  | 1 | 2 | 3 | 4 | 5 | 6 | 7 | 8 |
|---|---|---|---|---|---|---|---|---|
|  | F♯ | G♯ | A♯ | B | C♯ | D♯ | E♯ | F♯ |
| Right | 2 | 3 | 4 | 1 | 2 | 3 | 1 | 2 |
| Left | 4 | 3 | 2 | 1 | 3 | 2 | 1 | 4 |

## F♯/G♭ Major Scale

|  | 1 | 2 | 3 | 4 | 5 | 6 | 7 | 8 |
|---|---|---|---|---|---|---|---|---|
|  | G♭ | A♭ | B♭ | C♭ | D♭ | E♭ | F | G♭ |
| Right | 2 | 3 | 4 | 1 | 2 | 3 | 1 | 2 |
| Left | 4 | 3 | 2 | 1 | 3 | 2 | 1 | 4 |

# About The Author

## Why so many people learn music from Micah

The best instructors teach the student, not the curriculum. The curriculum serves as a vehicle for learning. It's a tool of sorts. One of the best parts of teaching music lessons–in this case, piano chording–is the ability to help a student learn at just the right pace. I've found that my job as an educator is to always be encouraging my students to take one step more than he or she may not have taken on their own. The only thing to sort out is at which pace each student performs best.

I've been teaching piano and guitar courses for more than ten years. My emphasis has always been, and will likely always be, in commercial music. While I think classical music is worth studying, I always find myself improvising over the original melodies–even those of the greats, like Beethoven, Brahms, or Bach. It's human nature to explore or be curious and I love teaching with the mindset that the music greats of the past are like proven guides. They shouldn't always be copied, but rather those from whom to learn.

Living twenty-five miles from downtown Nashville, TN has provided myself and family privileges in music that I'm certain are not given in every town. You can't throw a stone in Nashville without hitting someone who is personally or has a family member in the music industry. Not one of us takes the Grand Ole Opry backstage tour because we all plan to be there as an artist someday. Even if we sing and play music for Jesus as Christian or worship artists, we still likely won't spend the time or money for that tour. We plan to perform on that ageless circle that lands center-stage someday ourselves.

My wife of nearly ten years is glowing brighter every year. We have four kids who keep us very busy and tired. We also keep two Yorkshire Terrier dogs who I'm sure my wife would give away for less than the price of two movie tickets. I love them though.

It's an honor to help you work toward your piano chording goals. These new methods may unlock creativity in you that has been buried deep within for years. It's time to let it out.

Blessings,

-Micah Brooks
www.micahbrooks.com
Find me on Facebook, Twitter, LinkedIn, Instagram, and Amazon.com

# Connect With Micah Brooks

**Signup for Micah Brooks emails to stay up to date**

Subscribe to the Micah Brooks Company "Stay Connected" email list for the latest book releases. This email list is always free and intended to deliver high-value content to your inbox. Visit the link below to signup.

www.micahbrooks.com

**Contact Micah**

Email Micah Brooks at micahbrooks.com/contact. I want to know who you are. It's my privilege to respond to your emails personally. Please feel free to connect.

**Please share this book with your friends**

If you would like to share your thanks for this book, the best thing you can do is to tell a friend about *Piano Chords Two* or buy them a copy. You can also show your appreciation for this book by leaving a review on Amazon:

www.amazon.com

**Follow Micah Brooks:**

**Facebook:** @micahbrooksofficial
**Twitter:** @micahbrooksco
**LinkedIn:** Micah Brooks
**Instagram:** @micahbrooksco
**Amazon:** amazon.com/author/micahbrooks

If you have trouble connecting to any of these social media accounts, please visit www.micahbrooks.com.

Worship Publishing is a resource website that includes books, daily devotions, music, podcasts, product reviews, and many more recommendations. Use our wealth of staff writers and high-quality guest post content to better your walk with the Lord. This is the website where you can find publishing information for WorshipHeart Publishing, the publisher of this book.
Visit: www.worshippublishing.com.

Sing to him a new song;
play skillfully, and shout for joy.

Psalm 33:3 (NIV)

Made in the USA
Coppell, TX
10 October 2020